Leadership for Mental Wellbeing in the Secondary School

Leadership for Mental Wellbeing in the Secondary School is an introduction to a set of simple shifts you can enact to make your work more rewarding, and your school a flagship of excellence.

Full of practical tools and proven strategies, this book draws on a combination of research and experience to empower you to make confident changes on your own terms that are suitable for you and the unique circumstances of your school.

No matter what stage of your career, this book will help you:

- influence disenchanted and overloaded teaching staff to feel motivated and valued again (and improve the budgetary bottom line in the process)
- increase pupil confidence and resilience, preventing deeper mental health problems down the line
- practise bold leadership and deliver on what you really came into teaching for – preparing rounded, confident, individuals for life

Emphasising whole-person and whole-school approaches, this book is for any school leader looking to transform how they, their staff and their students feel about and cope with the day-to-day challenges and demands placed upon them.

Shirley Billson has spent more than a decade helping anxious young people and adults to overcome mental obstacles and thrive. She speaks regularly on topics including courage and motivation and how to challenge accepted norms to build self-esteem. She founded the Mental Wealth Factory in 2018 to support secondary schools and teens under pressure. However, since 2020, having identified the surprising parallels between anxiety in puberty and anxiety in midlife, she has dedicated the majority of her time to providing therapeutic coaching to adults in midlife and menopause through Menopause Anxiety Freedom.

Leadership for Mental Wellbeing in the Secondary School

Implementing Whole School Strategies

Shirley Billson

LONDON AND NEW YORK

First published 2022
by Routledge
4 Park Square, Milton Park, Abingdon, Oxon OX14 4RN

and by Routledge
605 Third Avenue, New York, NY 10158

Routledge is an imprint of the Taylor & Francis Group, an informa business

© 2022 Shirley Billson

The right of Shirley Billson to be identified as authors of this work has been asserted in accordance with sections 77 and 78 of the Copyright, Designs and Patents Act 1988.

All rights reserved. No part of this book may be reprinted or reproduced or utilised in any form or by any electronic, mechanical, or other means, now known or hereafter invented, including photocopying and recording, or in any information storage or retrieval system, without permission in writing from the publishers.

Trademark notice: Product or corporate names may be trademarks or registered trademarks, and are used only for identification and explanation without intent to infringe.

British Library Cataloguing-in-Publication Data
A catalogue record for this book is available from the British Library

Library of Congress Cataloging-in-Publication Data
Names: Billson, Shirley, author.
Title: Leadership for mental wellbeing in the secondary school: implementing whole school strategies / Shirley Billson.
Description: Abingdon, Oxon; New York, NY: Routledge, 2022.
Identifiers: LCCN 2021030999 (print) | LCCN 2021031000 (ebook) | ISBN 9781032157696 (hardback) | ISBN 9780367373832 (paperback) | ISBN 9780429353420 (ebook)
Subjects: LCSH: Educational leadership–Psychological aspects. | High school students–Mental health. | High school teachers–Mental health. | Education, Secondary–Social aspects. | Educational psychology. | School improvement programs.
Classification: LCC LB2806 .B55 2022 (print) | LCC LB2806 (ebook) | DDC 371.2/011–dc23
LC record available at https://lccn.loc.gov/2021030999
LC ebook record available at https://lccn.loc.gov/2021031000

ISBN: 978-1-032-15769-6 (hbk)
ISBN: 978-0-367-37383-2 (pbk)
ISBN: 978-0-429-35342-0 (ebk)

DOI: 10.4324/9780429353420

Typeset in Sabon
by Deanta Global Publishing Services, Chennai, India

Contents

Preface	**ix**
Introduction	**xiii**

1 The way it is: A cauldron for chronic stress   **1**

Long-term impact   1
Education or health responsibility?   2
Why grit isn't synonymous with mental well-being   2
Mental ill health: prevention vs. intervention   2
Is your agenda out of alignment?   3
The power of leadership   4
What we all really want   5
Understanding the mental wealth continuum   6
Not just about young people   7
Lacking control   8
In their own words   9
Belonging and inclusivity   10
Perfectionism and people pleasing   11
Data measurement   12
Parental involvement   12
Mental health in a box   13
Could you be wrong about their future?   13
Notes   14

2 Time for change   **15**

Education: serving an old model of the world?   15
The mental health impact of cognitive dissonance   16
Faulty goal setting and the impact on mental health   20
Performance gap and mental health   25
Performance gap and mental ill health   26
Your role as a pioneer   27
When best efforts aren't enough   27
Notes   29

3 Doing your best?   **31**

In their own words   32
Mental health: not your problem?   32
A simple one-step solution   33
Change your core policy and mission?   34

Contents

Practise what you preach   34
Responding to a moving landscape   36
Fixing broken people vs. enabling resilient people   37
Grades and pass rates   39
The dangers of box ticking   40
Staff well-being   40
Stress at work   41
In their own words   42
The pressure of observation   42
Teacher well-being   43
Prioritising data over learning   43
In need of a leader   43
The problem with continuing professional development (CPD)   44
The villainy of Ofsted and the DoE   45
Effective mental fitness initiatives?   46
Measurement and monitoring   47
Behaviour, exclusion and off-rolling   47
Mental health trends: children and young people   51
Mental health trends   52
Growth mindset: golden opportunity or fake news?   53
Current mental health tactics: the pick-and-mix approach   57
Seven common mental health intervention strategies and their value   60
Diversity, inclusivity and exclusions   62
Notes   65

4   Winning strategies   67

Start with you   68
The role of your reticular activating system (RAS) and mine!   70
Brain Function Summary (and its role in mental wealth/poverty)   71
Proven strategies   73
Culture change: quick fixes   74
The physiology of stress   74
Whole-school thinking   75
Looking for a framework?   76
Set a mental wealth strategy the lazy way   83
Why, who, when, where, what, how?   83
Make insignificant changes   87
Throw pebbles   87
Practise gratitude   88
The role of decision-making   89
Change the dialogue from what to who   90
Belonging and identity   91
Behaviour and identity   92
Mindful language   93
Focus on what works   94
Solution-focused practice   96
Ask a miracle question   97

vi

Contents

Avoid telling yourself or others to *not* do something or to *stop* doing
  something   98
Challenging Eeyore thinking   99
Learn to look for the detail in the solution   101
Mind your language   103
Final words   105
Notes   107

Preface

As a parent, I'm all too aware of the role schools and teachers play in building adolescent mental health. As a former complaints and communications senior manager in the National Health Service (NHS), I have had first-hand experience of local *Child and Adolescent Mental Health Services* (CAMHS) management and how often it fails young people. As a long-standing clinical hypnotherapist, good enough to be asked to run professional workshops for NHS clinical psychologists, I have personally worked with hundreds of distressed young people, let down by the healthcare system, and been privileged to learn what so many of them really feel about life, themselves and the relentless pressure of performance expectations. As a manager in a homeless charity, I have borne witness to the tragic impact of neglected mental health in adults and young people. As the founder of the Mental Wealth Factory, I have been invited to speak to secondary school staff and students on how to manage pressure and anxiety, have provided keynote motivational speaking on courage and resilience for Young Enterprise Gloucestershire and workshops for national Mental Health in Schools conferences, and have run workshops for parents of teens under pressure as a family learning tutor for Worcestershire County Council. My MA dissertation was on the export marketing of education and its contribution to a service-based economy.

I bring a unique and broad-based perspective on education, business and economy, mental health and young people that few specialists can match. My business experience encompasses recruitment advertising, digital and traditional marketing and communications, working within the NHS, local government and the charity sector – and informs my understanding of what the business world demands of school leavers. I have been the director of three businesses, as well as an entrepreneurial business coach, a digital marketer and a qualified solution-focused clinical hypnotherapist and psychotherapist. My teenage experience of depression, bullying and being the proverbial angry, sullen teenager inform my work, providing the connection that allows me to confidently help young people.

A personal perspective

My own teenage and life experience is one of the key drivers for why I believe so passionately in the change proposed throughout the pages of this book. I share my story, only to emphasise that it impacts on every strand and every moment of life.

Let me hasten to add that I had caring parents, lived in a safe neighbourhood and never went without. My background was most definitely lower middle class. However, I was a socially anxious and lonely child, happier clinging to my mother than taking part in any 'normal' childhood party games.

Preface

By the time I was 15 years old, I cried every night in my room but had no idea why. My mother took me to the GP, who prescribed anti-depressants. I didn't take them because I didn't like the way they flattened my mood and took away the highs as well as the lows. At 17, I took an overdose – but changed my mind in time to get myself to hospital. I was reviled by the nurses on the ward for being a 'time waster', taking a bed from a genuinely sick person.

Because of the overdose, I was compelled to see a psychiatrist. I saw her once and it was a waste of time. After all, I didn't have a Freudian condition ending in 'is' (neurosis, psychosis) and there wasn't a 'disorder' label they could attach.

I was subsequently bullied at 6th Form College and into my early twenties, so social anxiety remained an issue.

I kept my problems to myself, shared them with no one, acted like the bullying didn't bother me, even though I felt humiliated in front of friends. I learned how to feign popularity and mask hurt and I survived. So all's well that ends well, right? No. It isn't right. Because the impact of those years has reverberations that echo through the decades that follow.

Is any of this story familiar in the lives of today's young people? Sadly, yes. Was any of this the fault of my secondary school education? No. Absolutely not. Could it be changed for the better through *improved* secondary school education? Absolutely yes.

My life beyond school and why it's relevant to your mental health leadership

I entered an abusive relationship at 25, had career burnout at 28 and lost my career confidence at 30. Despite getting okay grades at school (mostly A's and B's), being a member of Mensa at age 21, getting a degree at 25 and then a master's in my thirties, most of my career has been a catalogue of underachievement. It has been a long, hard battle with life and myself, often feeling I was lacking or just not cut out for life and work.

I didn't have dyslexia, autism or behaviour issues; but I did have mental poverty (more on that later). I feared I was stupid, felt inferior to most others and got low from time to time. I also, regretfully, sometimes became the bully. A sad indictment on life for someone who's only real problem was to be from a lower middle–class background, with no access to successful role models, mentors, counsellors or coaches; and no understanding of how to truly build or evaluate any kind of emotional skill.

I was just an ordinary girl, not too much trouble, not excelling, but not failing either. Like so many students in your school, I fell through the cracks. Through all the experiences and training I've had since, I have come to realise that, with better mental wealth (see page) building strategies, my life and career could have been so much more rewarding and fulfilling with the right mental fitness education, information and guidance.

The truth is that my unfettered mental health lows and inadequate or non-existent teenage guidance meant performance has been impaired in *every* part of my life.

Let me stress that this isn't a 'poor me' fest. It is simply an example of the negative outcomes that can and do ensue if we fail to acquire the right type of mental fitness education during the childhood and adolescent years.

And the impact of failing to make emotional support and mental fitness skill development a higher priority than exam passes means we passively contribute to an increasingly

Preface

fractured and damaged society, where young people are not emotionally and mentally fit for the world in which they live and, ultimately, work.

Doom, gloom and disaster are not guaranteed, for sure. But don't we owe it to ourselves and to future generations to commit to continued learning about everything? Including mental fitness and ways to build it.

Introduction

What if there was a way you could be a better school leader; reduce staff turnover and absenteeism; lower levels of anxiety amongst students and staff; hit – or exceed – pass and grade targets; and have happy, supportive parents?

Would you sleep more soundly every night? Would you think it was possible?

Things you thought were impossible might just be possible

I believe it *is* possible and, throughout the pages of this book, I aim to lift the veil on the misinformation and limiting beliefs that hamper so many school leaders and policymakers, so that you can start to make very simple changes that will make your work more rewarding, and your school a flagship of excellence, that will delight everyone, from the governors to the parents, the teachers and the pupils.

It requires that you temporarily leave your objections at the door. Don't worry, you can collect them later if they remain that important to you. However, objections like, 'that won't work', 'that isn't possible here', 'it's way more complicated than that', 'it's out of my control', 'it's not my fault (it's Ofsted, the government or a.n.other)', 'I'm too busy', 'that's too simplistic', etc., will prevent you from benefitting from relatively minor shifts in thinking, behaviour and policy implementation. For now, though, I ask that you suspend all judgement and doubt.

This book is intended as so much more than a book about tweaking a few mental health policies and bolting on a bit of training. It's for anyone and everyone who is in a position to make a critical difference in the lives of young people, who risk experiencing all that I've experienced or worse, yet deserve so much better.

It is a starting point, not an end point, for positive change in school, at home and in work, during the school years and way beyond them. If you expect or demand that it remains firmly within the narrow remit of the mental health of young people, you will be rudely disappointed. The book may well seem presumptuous in its range. It is also about tough love (for you!).

Some of what I say – or, even much of what I say – may cause your hackles to rise. For some of you, your natural inclination may be to resist what I am saying, to object, to claim that your situation is different, or that I have no idea what I'm talking about because I am not on the frontline.

You may question why I devote whole sections to consider the wider implications of economic, technological, social and political change. It is because the interplay between

xiii

Introduction

each of these, the mission of your school and the mental well-being of everyone within it is intricately connected. Gaining a greater sense of the how and the why means you will think differently about every day-to-day decision, behaviour and conversation. Aligning this new awareness with the mental wealth building tools shared in these pages will transform the culture of your school, your own mental well-being and that of your staff and students.

I am hoping you picked up this book because you wanted things to change, because you were willing to consider that there could be a different way, because you are tired of firefighting, of staff leaving, of children suffering, of absenteeism, of struggle.

Who is this book for?

This book is for you if you're a new head wanting to make your mark and make a huge difference in the lives of your staff, your students and your entire school, including yourself. It's also for you if you're an existing head who's making great strides towards building a flagship school with a distinct emphasis on mental fitness, which includes an emphasis on whole-person and whole-school approaches. You know there's always more you can do, but it excites you rather than deflates you. Happy, well-rounded human beings are more important to you than any data collection expectations.

Who is this book *not* for?

This book is not for you if you're looking for a quick fix mental health policy that will rubber stamp your efforts and demonstrate to the outside world that you are 'doing something'. Having a policy has no connection with actually making a difference. This book is equally not for you if you think you have tried that, done that, bought the T-shirt and nothing really works anyway. It is not for you if you are planning to simply hand responsibility to your designated mental health lead, telling them to 'read that' so you can get on with the real job of school leadership.

You are the difference

This book speaks to the deepest part of you that drew you to want to teach in the first place, to make a positive difference in the lives of young people. I am genuinely on your side. It's just that, when it comes to achieving major breakthroughs of the kind you so desperately need and want for your school, the kind of feedback policies you might be familiar with – to highlight two things you've done well and one thing to improve on – won't deliver the impact or the results you or your school really deserve.

How this book might differ from others is that it builds on learning acquired over 15 years of private clinical practice, helping thousands of individuals to overcome anxiety and rebuild confidence. You might question the validity of this learning in a setting of 1000 students upwards. However, I have discovered that there is a powerful ripple effect which you cannot stop once you set it in motion. I have seen it played out like a gentle tsunami across every personal contact point in a person's life, from parents to employers, partners, colleagues and friends. Change one aspect of a single person's thinking and you influence everyone with whom they come into contact. Change the way a head teacher thinks and behaves and you change the school.

xiv

Introduction

My job is not to massage head teacher egos or join in a fanfare of agreement over how difficult things are, and how little control you have. Instead, it is to help you entertain the possibility that you genuinely can make the kind of big changes needed, that will put a halt to wrestling and wrangling with doubt and scepticism. Because once you accommodate the thought that the things you used to think were impossible might just be possible, you are just one small step from making that change. And if you can make such a major change in your own thinking, the school will most certainly get to benefit.

So, I have a question for you. Will you take on the challenge of thinking differently and embracing the possibility of big change? Yes? Congratulations! By opening the pages of this book and reading this far, you have made a start.

Now the courageous work begins.

What this book is and how to use it

Above all, this book is an introduction to – or an expansion of – a way of thinking, that can dramatically transform your own mental fitness and that of your entire school when fully understood. It is not a dogma and it does *not* provide training for identifying high-risk individuals or ways you can safeguard them. These aspects of mental fitness are well covered by others, including Mental Health First Aid England. Neither does it provide templates or toolsets that you can plug and play independently from a change in school cultural values. However, it does provide a core of learning and a way to connect the dots that empowers you to make confident changes on your own terms that are suitable for you and the unique circumstances of your school. It also seeks to identify how seemingly unconnected school policies impact, indirectly or directly, on the mental well-being of staff and students, so that you can make better-informed plans, judgements and decisions.

You and your own personal development of mental fitness skills are at the centre of everything. The book provides prompts and tools for thinking differently about every action you, or others, take that will either amplify mental resilience, self-belief and calm confidence, or diminish it. It asks you to question and challenge the status quo. This includes school rules, tradition, metrics, the way things are and the way things have always been. You will gain a greater understanding of what can work and what won't work on the basis of how the individual human brain works, rather than how policymakers imagine human beings function. The information shared in these pages is rooted more in modern studies of neuroscience and positive psychology, as it applies to individuals, rather than 20th-century social psychology which relies on aggregated norms and collective behaviour. Continued momentum is powered by a continual commitment to mental fitness above any other performance measure. Each of the tools and tips and the knowledge laid out in the pages of the book support you in this endeavour.

However, avoid selective reading. Read in its entirety for context. Then, evaluate which aspects have most relevance for your own school's unique make-up and circumstances. The whole point of the book is that there is no one-size-fits-all solution, but there are a set of simple shifts you can make to transform how you, your staff and your students feel day to day, and how they cope with the challenges and demands placed upon them.

xv

Chapter 1

The way it is

A cauldron for chronic stress

Like you, I am passionate about helping young people thrive as well-rounded, 'whole' people. This has to encapsulate building positive mental health, because long-standing evidence shows that mental health problems which begin in childhood continue in to adulthood Which means any individual gains in educational attainment, skill or knowledge, will be, at best, diminished by mental health limitations. At worst, they will impact on a person's ability to secure future education or employment worthy of them, to form positive long-term relationships and to be happy and successful on their terms. Ever.

LONG-TERM IMPACT

A growing body of evidence, mainly from high-income countries, has shown that there is a strong socio-economic gradient in mental health, with people of lower socio-economic status having a higher likelihood of developing and experiencing mental health problems

see www.mentalhealth.org.uk/statistics/mental-health-statistics-poverty

Results of the National Child Development Study (NCDS), a continuing, multidisciplinary longitudinal study, show a strong unfavourable correlation between childhood conduct disorder and

- qualifications and employment
- relationships and family formation
- health and disability by age 33

(Source: The Mental Health Foundation, Lifetime Impacts. Report of a seminar organised by the Office of Health Economics and the Mental Health Foundation, April 2004. See www.mentalhealth.org .uk/sites/default/files/lifetime_impacts.pdf.)

DOI: 10.4324/9780429353420-1

The way it is

Education or health responsibility?

The question, you might ask, reasonably, is whether the responsibility for the required improvements falls within the remit of education or health. For me, the answer is both. It is both unhelpful and, arguably, damaging for us, as a society, to separate responsibility for mental well-being and academic success as if, in some way, we could isolate parts of the human psyche, such that they have no impact on other parts.

A sense of identity, belonging, self-esteem, confidence and self-belief are the cornerstones of good mental health and a happy life. It isn't acceptable to simply enable academic success and think that's good enough, because this is no better than the over-zealous sports coach, who focuses so intently on winning the game or the race that the welfare of an athlete plays second fiddle.

Deep down you know this, but do your actions as a school leader actually reflect this?

Why grit isn't synonymous with mental well-being

Fortunately for me, I did have a kind of 'grit' that got me through it; however, despite the positive publicity that 'grit' gets, it isn't 'grit' that's needed. That's because grit is sometimes just another way of describing avoidance or suppression, and too many people become skilled at pretending it's all okay and even convince themselves that they really are when they're not. You see this very early on with young people. This book is not about short-term fixes. It is, instead, devoted to enabling you, your staff and your students to perform better, and feel better about life for the long term.

For me – and probably you – getting by or surviving isn't really what we want from life, or what we want for our young people. What we all need, in order to live and contribute to our fullest potential, is self-belief, self-esteem, confidence and a mindset for growth. This is a toolset that lasts for life, not just for schooldays!

My own sporting, relationship and academic potential were marred for too many years because no one ever taught me about the value of emotional intelligence, or confidence, or self-esteem, or a growth mindset.[1] I am aware that many people in education in the United Kingdom don't 'believe' in a growth mindset, like it's some kind of cult religion, rather than a valuable contribution to understanding psychological well-being. However, for me, there are some valuable takeaways if you take the time to forget the label and dig deep to understand what useful learning lies within this, which I'll refer to within the book.

Mental ill health: prevention vs. intervention

Everyone talks about mental health. Yet, most of the time they're really talking about mental ill health. The focus of intent for solutions and ways to improve the situation are all about managing, treating or preventing mental ill health. Like molehills, though, more and more examples of mental ill health in young people are cropping up on a seemingly daily basis; self-harm, anxiety, eating disorders, gambling addiction, depression, body dysmorphia, to name a few. Other 'conditions' will no doubt have been reported in the press and clinicians will continue to pathologise stress-related problems as something bigger. Which is not to suggest I'm trivialising the severity of any of these conditions. On the contrary, they are, in my view, distressing symptoms of wider ills within our society, some of which I intend to be bold enough to address within the confines of this book. However, because the emphasis is on mental ill health and the wide variety of specific conditions, it can be easy to get caught up in it. As an education professional, you may find yourself being asked to respond differently to each of these fresh problems as they assert themselves.

Even though it is well known that poor mental health affects performance, secondary school solutions are rarely anything more than a mixed bag of piecemeal add-ons.

Understandably, as a busy head, you may delegate the responsibility for sourcing solutions and delivering relevant teaching, usually to someone on your existing teaching staff. You may designate a mental health lead – or appoint specific individuals to counsel, coach and support the pupils in your care. You provide good, old-fashioned pastoral care, only now it seems to be on steroids.

Homespun solutions proliferate, some of which can be pretty impressive. However, it isn't systematic and it depends on the energy and commitment of a dedicated few. This means it's hard to replicate. When key people leave, successful 'systems' flounder, stagnate or die.

The original pastoral care you had in place may seem insufficient, stretched at the seams, to manage the scale and severity of mental ill health problems now presented. So you task your team with suggestions for bolstering it and you send members of the senior leadership team (SLT) to conferences and training, so they can impart fresh learning on exactly how to improve the way your school manages the problem (without too much added expense). Those fortunate enough to attend the training are expected to distil their learning into knowledge they can transfer to colleagues. This reflects the wider pattern of education.

Great teaching rests too often in the hands of dedicated individuals, not great leaders. Unsurprisingly, great mental health education also rests in the hands of dedicated individuals, not great leaders. Worse still, some school leaders actually hinder well-being initiatives by limiting their application beyond Year 10. After all, time spent on well-being is 'spare' time, better used for increased General Certificate of Secondary Education (GCSE) teaching. The thinking being, that pupils' exam performance and outcomes beyond the school gates, are always better enhanced by more subject teaching and not by greater emphasis on teaching young people how to use their minds more effectively for long-term learning and resilience.

Mental health difficulties amongst young people, including self-harm and suicide, are high profile and on the increase (NHS DIGITAL, 2018[2]), with under-resourcing from the National Health Service (NHS) to deal with this. Parents and schools experience the fallout, with secondary schools expected to effectively identify, support and manage young people with mental health problems. Often, head teachers, parents and young people feel afraid, ill-equipped and, in some cases, resentful.

Is your agenda out of alignment?

Yet whilst much gnashing of teeth and hand-wringing is devoted to questioning the 'right' thing to do to stem this tsunami of mental health crises in young people, a conversation with almost any teacher – or, more likely, any ex-teacher – will tell you that too few secondary schools put mental well-being at the top of the agenda. Despite the fact that rising mental ill health in young people has obvious short-term impacts on exam performance, attendance and behaviour, all of which are significant data measures of success, the relentless demand for data continues.

The way it is

School management, instead, is dominated by spreadsheets, grades and percentage pass rates. Although there may be a box checked that confirms there is a mental health policy, available on the school website, there is little evidence of a powerful mental well-being strategy at the heart of many a school culture. Mental well-being can seem like a nice to have, but not a must have. If you can't data gather it, you can't do anything about it – or so it can seem.

I believe it is no coincidence that much of the teaching profession is claiming under-funding, overburdened workloads and poor appreciation – and they are leaving the profession in droves. Students are under pressure, teachers are under pressure. There seems to be little room for innovation, creativity, flexibility and, dare I say it, *fun*, in the classroom – at least not beyond Year 10. Teachers and students are straitjacketed and shoe-horned into a way of working not designed for individuals, but for number crunching.

Mental poverty (see p. 15) seems to have become a natural by-product of modern life and the way we live it. The therapeutic, pharmaceutical and healthcare answers we are being offered do nothing but provide a sticking plaster over the crack in the dam that is close to bursting.

Why? In my opinion, it is a clashing combination of 20th-century thinking – which meant that educational achievement would enable us to be in command of our own economic destiny – and the 21st-century explosion of the internet and social media, demonstrating that economic freedoms can be won in other ways than movement through an educational or professional hierarchy. Education has become no guarantee of work, security or income. In this brave new world, we are also discovering that economic freedom may not be the only answer we seek.

It's possible that your definitions of mental well-being are out of alignment too. These days, teachers and journalists may talk about 'grit' and 'resilience', instead of a 'stiff upper lip'. However, whilst that 'stiff upper lip' may have had a rebrand in terminology, it's the same old expectation that we learn how to contain our emotion, rather than learn what to do with that emotion so we can build a store of mental wealth. It remains an endemic way of thinking, behaving and educating. It's time for a better understanding of what resilience really is and that means a fundamental shift – leadership by example.

The power of leadership

Mental health leadership is so much more than having a mental health policy in place for students. It's also, vitally, about you, the leader. The question is, have you put your own house of mental fitness in order?

Individually, we are only ever in control of ourselves and what we do, with little impact on our external environment. As a head teacher, you have extended powers conferred upon you. You can both impact what you do for yourself and your own mental well-being, as well as alter the mental health environment your students and staff inhabit for so much of the year.

Radical thinking and courageous, innovative leadership can be the catalyst for positive school-wide change. Student and staff mental health are correlated, so it is imperative that you explore co-ordinated strategies for improving both student and staff well-being. Effective mental health planning and leadership can deliver massive cost–benefit in terms of reduced absenteeism and exclusion of young people, as well as reduced absenteeism and turnover of staff. Think of the money that could be saved in supply teaching, and the reduction in disruption from staff turnover, if teachers weren't so persistently overwhelmed, demoralised and demotivated. Maybe they would stay in love with the vocation they chose for longer than the current average of 5 years from graduation.

It astonishes me that there appears to be no single strategy currently available for schools that guides them in how to manage rising mental health issues in young people *and* how to simultaneously stem the tide of teachers leaving the profession. The two are most definitely correlated. Improve one and you will see improvement in the other. Consciously work to improve both and I believe you will reap exponentially greater rewards in terms of achievement and budget.

I hope, within the confines of this book, to share tools, strategies and practices that will help you to be at the forefront of change. I share the underpinning neuroscience and psychology to help you improve understanding of your own mental health, as well as that of the young people in your school, and to be better informed about ways you could use that knowledge to improve staff well-being too.

Improvements are not achieved solely by increasing medication or access to counsellors and other mental health practitioners, nor by expecting the NHS to deal with the detritus contributed to by the environment and out-of-step parenting or education – but by being the source of positive change, by becoming the new way.

My aim is that you enjoy the ride, and that you start to feel more motivated and engaged in the positive leadership of your school than you may have done in a very long time.

I believe there is a way to benefit the entire school organisation (staff and students) in a way that increases self-esteem, resilience, motivation, happiness *and* performance at school and way beyond the school gates.

WHAT WE ALL REALLY WANT

I'd like to borrow a quote from Dr Michael Peterson, co-director of the Whole Schooling Consortium in America. It underpins the tenet of this book:

> The fact is that most parents and educators, when clearly asked, do not want education for work as the prime outcome of schooling. They want much more. We often conduct workshops with educators and parents in which we ask them to describe what has made the best year and the worst year for children. Always, teachers and parents state that what made the difference lay more in how the student was treated and positive or negative relationships rather than how well they did on particular tests. In other words, in addition to cognitive learning of basic skills and even critical thinking skills, the emotional and social well-being of the child is paramount. Helping children develop in these arenas is a key expectation and goal for most people.
>
> (Source: Michael Peterson, 2009. WholeSchooling.ne t. See www.wholeschooling.net/WS/WSPrncples/WS %200%20purpose%20schls.html)

The way it is

A big ask? A utopian dream? I don't think so

There is the chance for courageous, innovative head teachers, policymakers and mental health leads to make a dramatic difference to the mental fitness of a generation, to become thought leaders themselves and to change the direction of education to better meet the needs of all students – to become well-rounded, satisfied and fulfilled human beings.

And isn't that what teachers have always wanted, their key motivation for teaching?

Understanding the mental wealth continuum

Mental health is not an on/off switch. It is not something you either have or don't have. It is, instead, a continuum between extremes of mental dysfunction and optimum levels of mental fitness. Mental poverty sits at one end of the spectrum and mental wealth at the other.

Every single one of us sits somewhere on this spectrum. Every single one of us could face an experience or a series of experiences that move us from a place of relative mental health and well-being to a place of mental ill health. In other words, we are *all* at risk and nobody is either entirely free of any mental health challenges, or wholly 'broken'.

Too often, we hear mental fitness described as mental health. And many of us infer that if we are not diagnosed with some form of mental ill health or if we are holding our lives together relatively well, then we are, by default, mentally well. And we make the same faulty assessment of others.

Nothing could be further from the truth. It is a rare person (possibly nobody) who suffers with no mental health challenges. Sure, many of us can hold down jobs, show up at school, laugh with friends and, outwardly, perform well. However, for most of us, our state of mental health isn't something that's obvious to read on the outside.

We all hear reports of shocked relatives who experience suicide in the family. 'There was no sign', or 'they seemed happy', 'nothing seemed to be worrying him/her' are the common phrases. The truth is that, for the majority of young people and adults falling into any kind of chronic mental ill health that requires specialist diagnosis or treatment, there is no obvious warning sign. Sure, we can be trained to look for changes in behaviour, but it is easy for some children (and adults) to smile and seem happy on the outside when they are crumbling on the inside. In fact, they may convince themselves that this is an easier and 'safer' route than letting anyone know there could possibly be anything the matter.

I use the analogy with wealth because it seems more helpful than the current relatively fixed view that we are either mentally fit or mentally unwell. This leads to unhelpful judgement of self and others – and a failure to recognise when change or support is required and when it isn't, or even what type of change or support might be appropriate.

When it comes to money, we understand that there are extremes of wealth and poverty, and we also understand that there are many points on a sliding scale where we might sit. Some points might be more comfortable than others. Equally, one person will feel satisfied at a level where another person feels uncomfortable. Some will strive constantly for more and never feel that what they have is enough. Others will find contentment with relatively little.

Like a black to white continuum, there can be a plethora of shades of grey in between. And it helps to appreciate this. Mental wealth is not an absolute that you have or do not have. It is as much about personal perception of your own position on a scale of

6

well-being as something somebody else decides for you. Importantly, it can apply equally to organisations and people.

One of the core influencing factors in moving up and down the spectrum is the experience of chronic stress, which has become prevalent in modern life. Throughout the book, we evaluate what factors contribute to this prevalence and how to change thought processes to maintain a sense of calm control, no matter what happens.

Like physical health, some might be perceived as fitter than others; however, just as there are multiple measures of physical fitness, there are multiple measures of mental fitness. Like some physical illness, it's not always obvious on the outside what ails someone on the inside.

Some might be devoid of apparent illness (and, arguably, mentally fit) and seem quietly diligent, but suffer inwardly with low self-esteem (mental poverty indicator). Others might seem outwardly confident, yet, inwardly, they are terrified of failure (mental poverty indicator). They may get expert at avoidance strategies (mental poverty indicator) which prevent their perceived sense of inadequacy (mental poverty indicator) being exposed in specific situations. Others still might seem to lack consistent concentration and focus (mental poverty indicators) yet achieve high levels of exam – or occupational – performance.

Never confuse outward expressions of behaviour, or 'personality', with an evaluation of someone's relative state of mental wealth

As you read through the book, keep in mind an image of a simple mental wealth continuum. Diminishing and negative thought processes and uncomfortable emotions sit at one end of the spectrum and expansive or positive thought processes and uplifting emotions sit at the other. Keeping it simple in this way will help you to navigate your journey to cultivating an improved journey for yourself, and a better environment for everyone else. It will help you identify areas where improvements can be made, both on an individual and an aggregated scale. Even deep-seated, systemic issues that can lie at the heart of a young person's mental poverty, can be improved with the right listening and appropriate responses.

However, please do not assume that you are now tasked with preventing, fixing or ameliorating every single negative emotion, thought or experience. Of course not. Simply being mindful of the continuum is a huge step forward in making a big difference.

So, it is deeply unhelpful and prejudicial to regard someone as mentally fit just because they do not appear mentally unwell. It does little to encourage us to become better acquainted with our own place on the spectrum and to learn how to maintain or improve our own mental fitness, so we can move to higher levels on the spectrum, should we choose to. Equally, we are ill-equipped to develop mentally healthy organisations and environments if we have poor levels of understanding – or even acknowledgement of a mental well-being spectrum.

Not just about young people

It is a mistake to assume that the only demographic group to experience elevated levels of poor mental health are the young. Changes to society, personal expectations and workplace demands mean we all seem to struggle more than we once did – and, again, like physical illness, from time to time we are below par. Sometimes we self-heal and

The way it is

sometimes we need varying degrees of external help. The Covid-19 pandemic has made many of us more acutely aware of this than ever.

It's vital to understand this. Your responsibility as a school leader is to both staff and students. It is also to yourself. But the relentless impact of external events – economic, technological, environmental, social – means you have to acquire new skills to maintain your own mental fitness and to create places of work and study that cultivate ideal circumstances not just for maintaining mental health, but also for building reserves of mental wealth and moving from places of mental poverty now, and in the future. For everyone.

Growth of chronic stress

Any form of uncomfortable emotion is a psychological and physiological source of stress. Acute stress is good for us and helps strengthen our immune system (which is why activities like daily cold showers and cold water swimming are becoming increasingly popular). Chronic stress, however, is the precursor to both physical and mental ill health and most definitely puts us down the mental poverty end of the spectrum. Officially, stress is defined as externally generated and anxiety is internally generated.[3] However, if we have no access to understanding effective ways to deal with external stress, it becomes inevitable that anxiety will follow.

The rise of mental poverty

It may seem obvious to state that the world we now live in differs dramatically from the one my generation grew up in. In just the past 20 years alone, we have seen not just the beginnings, but the ubiquity of the internet, the launch and proliferation of social media channels and the smartphone, and now a pandemic and global concern for the state of the planet and the environment.

We have also experienced growing – and obvious – signs of material poverty, expressed in the growth of homelessness and food banks, no longer just in major cities but also in towns, large and small, the length and breadth of the United Kingdom. We have seen an escalation in knife crime and drug abuse, and the growth of county lines – again, edging from major cities to towns and even rural villages. Many young people are exposed, more commonly than any generation before them, to gangs, to organised crime and to sexual and criminal grooming. It may be they become at risk of drug abuse or crime themselves – or they have parents, friends or relatives involved; increasing the risk to a young person's personal well-being, whether they are directly involved or not. Because they lack control of their environment, this can lead them to doubt they have *any* control of their lives. Schooling and education can become an irrelevance. 'What's the point?' is an understandable response. For many, their environment means they deal with raised stress, anxiety and fear on a daily basis. Add to that the fact that the adolescent brain lacks good 'consequential' thinking. In other words, physiologically, they are less able to quickly evaluate the long-term consequences of risky actions. It isn't because they are wilfully stupid or simply badly behaved. Their brains genuinely lack this capacity until later in life.[4]

Lacking control

I'm not talking about classroom control, but about the vital need for young people to feel some sense of personal control and self-determination over their lives and their futures. Without this, hopelessness can take root and become a breeding ground for internal

8

discontent. This puts them at risk of long-term mental health difficulties. It is a key component of mental poverty. If you do not feel in control of your own life, what *are* you in control of? But it's not just children from underprivileged environments at risk.

Young people, fortunate enough to live in neighbourhoods or families where risks associated with material poverty are lower, often experience restricted freedoms not associated with previous generations. They are cosseted and 'protected' by being ferried to and from one another's homes, to and from school and to and from a plethora of extra-curricular activities. On the surface, it would seem churlish to criticise this level of privilege and protection borne out of caring. However, over-protected young people not only lose the ability to make good decisions for themselves, but they also lose any sense of control in their own lives. When every decision, large or small, appears to be taken for them in the interests of safety or physical well-being, as they enter adolescence, their innate drive for identity and self-affirmation is confused. Their ability to build skill in decision-making and gain confidence in taking on more control of their life, as required of normal progress to adulthood, is hampered by a sense (and reality) of lacking any real control over any aspect of their lives, which can be felt just as keenly as the child from an economically or socially deprived area. However, because of their apparent wealth of material advantage, their struggle with self-determination is commonly misinterpreted as a weakness. In truth, this lack of any sense of control in life is a core element of enduring mental poverty. Yet, social media feeds and mainstream media alike publicly criticise such young people as lacking grit or resilience and refer to them as the 'snowflake' generation. This is deeply unwarranted. It harms their mental fitness and increases their mental poverty. Every adolescent fibre of their being requires an assertion of self and the early stretching of boundaries that will help form the framework for their future adult life, laying foundation stones for relationships, friendships, careers and preferred lifestyle.

The same worrisome problem exists for isolated young people living in deprived environments or impoverished neighbourhoods with a weakened community and support network. Too many outwardly well-adjusted children are compelled to make daily choices that might involve gang membership, knife crime, gun crime, prostitution, drug dealing or even death. So, when well-meaning teachers lead them to believe there is only one way out of their environment – to pass these exams or stay stuck for ever – the pressure is intense. Imagine someone telling you that, as in the words of the Eminem song, you had just one shot at life and that the 'wrong' choice would end all choices? Any likelihood of achieving freedom and opportunity can seem entirely out of reach.

As an adolescent, belonging and identity are top of any list of priorities. A young person's identity is easily shaped by the path of least resistance. If it feels safer or easier to belong to a gang, rather than find the strength of will to ignore the daily presence of gang members on their street, or taunts on the way to school, it's an understandable choice. Belonging is everything and if school seems like a place where other pupils or teachers live on another distant planet, then it will also be the most logical choice. Not feeling a strong sense of belonging or shared identity creates a shaky foundation for mental wealth building.

In their own words

Anonymous Year 11

It's hard to concentrate at school – I just want to be liked. Teachers really don't get it. Some mean well, but they just don't understand. It feels like I can't really trust

The way it is

anyone. I wish there was someone I could trust, open up to, have a bond with, someone who knows exactly what I mean because they've been in that situation.

I've never felt safe. I need to have my walls up. It always feels like I have to be distant with people. I find it hard even to talk to friends. Teachers cannot understand unless they've been in my situation. Teachers don't understand that maybe it's something else that's bothering us when they're punishing or putting us in to detention. They should try to understand us, not punish us. School should be an oasis of safety, calm, trust, close friendships. And how can studying for GCSEs change all the bad stuff happening in the world – or prepare me for real life?

Social media can be positive when used for connection through messaging, access to help for loneliness, depression and anxiety... to be able to speak to friends even when we can't be together in person. Social media can help spread the word of positive engagement – e.g., GoFundMe able to help others. But, overall, I think social media is negative.

If influencers were willing to share that this was not their real life, share what their lives are really like – where they go, what they eat, how they dress, who they're with, it might be better. Endorsements should be chosen with more care – maybe the products they promote are bad for others – and they are only doing it for the money. They're making money from our loneliness and our sleep deprivation. Yet, aspirations are to be influencers, YouTubers.

I can be around 1000s of people but still feel alone. All these workshops don't stop us feeling alone, especially growing up in an area where there are stabbings. We can only rely on one person – ourselves. We don't feel safe or protected enough to talk to anyone. Everyone is for themselves.

Only a few teenagers have the courage to talk to someone. We can't trust anyone. I need to find someone open and engaging – not all teachers are.

Belonging and inclusivity

Standing out or being different is perceived as a threat by the primitive brain. So, if we feel isolated or different often enough, this will eventually lead to chronic stress. When we experience chronic stress, we also experience repetitive firing of the fight, flight or freeze response, flooding the brain and the body too often with adrenaline and cortisol and inhibiting the production of serotonin and dopamine, our natural mental wealth building armoury (for naturally induced feelings of calm and reward). It's another layer in the mental poverty tinder box, which can result in chronic or social anxiety, panic attacks, self-harm, angry outbursts, poor behaviour, etc.

Belonging and inclusivity are powerful drivers in building mental wealth or becoming stuck in mental poverty. To feel a sense of belonging, you don't need everyone to be like you, or think like you. But you do need to feel understood, to feel some sense of commonality, of shared interest or characteristics. Sharing a school uniform or the same teachers as everyone else doesn't fully cut it if you feel like you're different.

Despite the intense media coverage of mental health, the proliferation of mental health charities and high-profile public admissions of vulnerability or mental ill health, it can still be a source of deep shame for a young person in the midst of their teens, feeling like they might not fit in or conform – whether it's to the expectations of their peer group, their parents, teachers, some other person or environment where they feel it's important, or simply to their personal definition of 'normal'.

The way it is

It's that 'personal' definition which is so vital to understand. Our sense of 'normal' or belonging, our sense of being like others, or not like others, is internal. It is something we feel and we believe. It is not something that somebody else defines for us. It's based on our interpretation of what people say, how they say it, our reading of expressions and behaviours, of dress and every subtle nuance which we internalise as 'like us' or 'not like us'.

You might argue that this is the whole point of school uniform, or school mottos, or school rules, and that these become the shared identity everyone can buy into, without exception. The trouble is that this form of contrived commonality was established in a century when diversity within a school – or in society – was minimal. Most people looked like one another and sounded like one another. They had similar aspirations, came from similar social backgrounds and lived in similar houses with similar parents doing similar things. Nowadays, we live in a cosmopolitan and richly diverse society. Even in catchment areas with apparently limited diversity, there will be young people aware of their 'difference' based on what they see and hear in social media feeds.

Even if you believe your school is successful in fostering a sense of belonging, remember that is also a 'belief'. What we think we do and what we really do can be entirely different beasts. Unconscious bias is real and it is through unconscious bias, rather than intention, that your school culture, as expressed by every member of staff and young person within it, may be perpetuating a sense of exclusion and lack of belonging by encouraging a type of conformity and uniformity that is not necessary, or helpful, or valid.

There is a fine line between creating rules and boundaries within which a young person can feel supported and safe, and creating a straitjacket of illogical conformity, arguably better suited to the needs of a prison or place of correction.

Maybe it's time to re-evaluate those rules and regulations and question whether they are really doing the job they are intended to do, or if there is a better way. However much you might defend your school's record on inclusivity, if exam performance, behaviour management and grades remain the priority measures of success, then mental well-being will suffer.

Perfectionism and people pleasing

Some of the young people most surprisingly at risk in this environment are the people-pleasers, the children who fit in, go with the flow, don't rock the boat. To all intents and purposes, they are model children, always eager to please, to do what's expected of them and to succeed. These children are often high achievers too.

The difficulty is that they have no idea how to say no, how to express their doubt and fear. They fear letting others down. Instead, they unwittingly over-burden themselves, strive for perfection and constant praise, without which they feel inadequate and have a sense that their lives are out of control. They sacrifice their own mental health at the altar of parental ambition or school objectives to meet targets and to stand out with more top grades and pass rates. They can become slaves to parental ambition and unimaginative school leadership.

In order to feel any sense of control and predictable emotional security in their lives, they may become prone to conditions or disorders where control is an intrinsic aspect. This includes self-harm, eating disorders and obsessive compulsive disorder (OCD). Feeling unable to influence their own lives other than by meeting the standards and ideals of others, they seek to express themselves by exerting control in the only ways they perceive as open to them.

The way it is

Whilst this appears to make no logical sense to most adults, it makes perfect sense to those young people, crippled by the curse of perfectionism. On the outside, perfectionism might seem like a small flaw – and, arguably, a preferable one to disengagement or rebellion expressed as disruptive or disaffected behaviour. However, perfectionism is another tell-tale characteristic of mental poverty, cleverly hidden or obscured behind pleasing smiles and an obliging demeanour. Young people at some of the highest fee-paying schools experience this at almost epidemic proportions and, sadly, many high academic achieving academies mirror this. Yet, the leadership of such a school can be easily seduced by the gratifying display of top grades and high pass rates. Why would you seek to question or change anything? As the saying goes, 'If it ain't broke, don't fix it'. The point, however, is that it *is* broken.

Data measurement

We have become a society that has to measure everything. We are data obsessed, looking for trends, norms, changes from the norm, impact of policy. As a society, we seek the answers to all of our problems through data analysis.

In some cases, this makes perfect sense. Aggregated data can highlight trends that slip by unnoticed by a casual observer. Such data can highlight meaningful change – and drive early action – on occasion. We see this played out in environmental science, for example, highlighting seemingly small shifts in human behaviour, consumption and production that have large impacts on the life and climate of the planet. In this way, it helps us to become adept at using and interpreting data.

If we are being generous in our assumptions, data collection in schools is in the interests of the school's common good. There is aggregation, but there is also an intended connection with the individual for the greater well-being of that individual. Some data management systems even acknowledge and harness the widespread use of handheld technology and apps, by linking systems of behaviour management to communicate with parents and with class teachers. This moves beyond simple data collection to data communication. There is some positive benefit in this – especially when the data gathering improves the relationship between parent and school.

However, data collection and management that relates to the behaviour of young people on a personal level can be problematic – the tip of an iceberg that is an early concession to handing over our right to privacy, our right to identity and our right to object. Using data to draw conclusions about a person's behaviour, potential or likely performance outcomes risks attaching labels to individuals. Again, be mindful of unconscious bias here. You and your staff might think you're above attaching labels, but your unconscious mind beats to a different drum! Those labels can lead to judgement and stigma. In turn, this can foster resentment, damage self-esteem and increase self-doubt. Unsurprisingly, it's also likely to result in long-term underperformance, which gives the lie to corroborating the original data. It's another stone in the foundation of mental poverty.

Parental involvement

Parents of secondary school children commonly feel uninvolved with what happens to their child during the school day – and can feel undervalued, disengaged and resentful that their only contact or request for contribution from the school amounts to contact relating to their child's alleged poor behaviour, invites to parent's evenings or letters from the school seeking money for some trip or project. Those feelings of resentment, or worse, will influence how a child feels and the likely outcome, in terms of building chronic stress, is not good. They will either share the parental perspective, becoming challenging at school, or they will be caught between two stools, feeling like it is their responsibility to make things 'right', or to appease the adults in their lives. It isn't, and it never should be, their responsibility to make things right for any of us.

Disengagement and resentment are a poor foundation for fostering positive collaborative relationships. Yet, those relationships can and should, wherever possible, lie at the heart of much improvement in the health and well-being of the young people in your school.

Sure, you might have a care worker in the school who takes on the role of fostering closer relations with 'problem' children and their parents; however, that role either doesn't always exist (easy target for budget cuts) or is inadequately resourced to support *all* the children and parents requiring that level of contact.

Mental health in a box

One of the biggest problems in the way schools, policymakers and even mental health professionals approach mental health improvements is that they compartmentalise them in the same way everything else in a school is compartmentalised, into a department or a subject area, a specialism, as if you can neatly consign mental health to one part of the day, or one aspect of thinking and behaving. This is a fundamental flaw in the approach to making positive changes in schools. Mental health and well-being is not something you choose to experience or not. It is something you live, something you have and something you are. That includes all of us.

Could you be wrong about their future?

I want to share with you a quote (Daniel Priestley, *Key Person of Influence*, 2014, Rethink Press) which provides some insight into what I'm describing:

> Already we are seeing people as young as twenty making six-figure incomes with their ideas.
>
> Most people think that these 'whiz kids' are succeeding because they are good with technology, but this is not the whole story.
>
> These teenagers aren't attached to the idea that a business has to be the way it used to be. They don't think a brand has to cost a lot of money or that they have to live in a particular location in order to do business there. They don't think that their idea needs to please everyone or that they need to meet their clients face to face in order to deliver a powerful experience.
>
> That's why they are succeeding: not because they are better at using the technology, but because they are better at letting go of the way things were done in the past and probably because they were never attached to these ideas in the first place.

The way it is

Notes

1 For those interested in learning more about the original research underpinning growth mindset, I recommend reading Carol Dweck's *Mindset: Changing the Way You Think to Fulfil Your Potential*, 2012, Robinson. For a range of free, downloadable tools you can use to support you in the classroom and remotely, see www.mindsetworks.com.
2 https://digital.nhs.uk/news-and-events/latest-news/one-in-eight-of-five-to-19-year-olds-had-a-mental-disorder-in-2017-major-new-survey-finds.
3 www.mentalhealthfirstaid.org/external/2018/06/stress-vs-anxiety.
4 'In an fMRI study that investigated the neural mechanisms that might account for differences between adolescents and adults in decision-making, participants were presented with one-line scenarios (e.g. "Swimming with sharks") and were asked to indicate via a button press whether they thought this was a "good idea" or a "not good idea" (Baird, Fugelsang, & Bennett, 2005). There was a significant group by stimulus interaction, such that adolescents took significantly longer than adults on the "not good idea" scenarios relative to the "good idea" scenarios' (Source: Sarah-Jayne Blakemore and Suparna Choudhury, Development of the adolescent brain: implications for executive function and social cognition. *Journal of Child Psychology and Psychiatry* 47:3/4 [2006], pp. 296–312).

Chapter 2

Time for change

Education: serving an old model of the world?

Despite best intentions, I believe that many secondary schools are failing our young people – and, more than that, they risk failing society in the 21st century. We are in the midst of an economic revolution of equivalent impact to the Industrial Revolution. Even the millennial generation will soon lag behind the pace of change. Academic targets and traditional career ambitions are the stuff of yesteryear, suitable for a 20th-century world that changed slowly, that required consistency and structure, order and conformity, rules and replication. Yet, policymakers and many educators are steadfastly holding on to old ideals of examination success and academic performance as the gold standard of aspiration and wholly suitable measures of success. They may sincerely believe this is the way to develop well-rounded individuals. In reality, they are encouraging conformity to an outdated norm.

The 21st-century model of the world demands creative, independent thinking and an alacrity to thrive in a landscape of rapid change. Disruptive businesses, which challenge old standards and rule sets, are now the vanguard of business organisation. Conformist thinking is the antithesis of what this style of business demands of its employees.

Twenty-first-century people want personal freedom to express themselves, to confidently be whom they choose to be, without hindrance, prejudice or barriers. Yet, in school, we unconsciously expect young people to negate their sense of frustration, to quell their challenges to school norms, to block their internal questioning that something is not quite right. We ask them, still, to do as they are told, not as they believe. This is based on the old 20th-century premise that our elders know better, that youth is reckless and naïve and, let loose, will wreak havoc upon the world. The old way (stiff upper lip) requires that young people should be educated to control their emotions, rather than learn how to express them. It is out of step with what the world demands and what the world offers.

This way of educating is increasing mental poverty by fostering internal dissonance (see page 33) in young people. They live in an external world which bears no relation to that which exists within the confines of the school gates.

DOI: 10.4324/9780429353420-2

15

Time for change

Michael Peterson makes the point well:

> Two primary opposing views exist regarding the purpose of schools. Some, such as the Business Roundtable (A. Ryan, 2004) and Achieve (Achieve, 2004), an organization created by governors and business leaders, believe that the primary purpose of schools should be to create workers who have skills and personal styles to fill and perform available jobs. Others believe this outcome is too narrow (Freeman, 2005; Goodlad, 1984; Hodgkinson, 2006; Postman, 1996). For them schools should seek to develop active citizens, helping children develop their own capacity for personal achievement and contributing to society as an active citizen for democracy.
>
> And none of this equips young people for the 21st century model of the world, which demands creative, independent thinking and an alacrity to thrive in a landscape of rapid change.
>
> In so doing, I believe they are blocking the positive human development of a growing minority – the vanguard of this new revolution – creative young people who are thwarted by the demand that they conform, that they bend to the old order, that they deny the essence of who they are, or that they become like us and not like themselves.[1]

If you also factor in the growth of artificial intelligence, which will rapidly replace old information or system-based jobs and professions, the remaining advantage that human beings have to offer is creativity and individuality. A well-designed machine will always be more accurate, more reliable and more productive than even the most detail-oriented, diligent and information-rich person. Young people going into the world of work in the next 5, 10 or 15 years will need to excel at the pursuit of creativity and individuality in order to survive and thrive. Robots and modern variations of robots will replace the roles that 20th-century society created. We need to somehow find a way to encourage that pursuit of difference, whilst maintaining the human desire to network and engage socially – and for individuals to feel a part of something, a belonging.

Thought leaders from around the world are calling for change. Seth Godin and Ken Robinson,[2] for example, agree that the current system of education was designed in the industrial age to churn out factory workers. We send children to school to prepare for the real world. Yet, that real world is changing very fast and the fundamentals of education have changed little. Despite changes in curriculum and pedagogy, these are little more than cosmetic adjustments masquerading as fundamental shifts. This industrial age mentality of mass production and mass control still runs deep in schools.

The mental health impact of cognitive dissonance

You might be wondering what on earth any of this has to do with mental health or wellbeing. I have one term for you. Cognitive dissonance. If we educate young people in an environment that does not reflect the one they see or experience elsewhere (at home, on the street and online), then we potentially set them up to experience cognitive dissonance. The Merriam-Webster dictionary describes cognitive dissonance as 'psychological conflict resulting from incongruous beliefs and attitudes held simultaneously'. It is typically experienced as psychological distress when you participate in an action that goes against one or more of your contradictory values. So, if education tells you that

Time for change

one version of the world is real, but life experienced tells you another, you either have to choose which version to believe, or attempt to believe both. This is deeply uncomfortable and a perfect bedrock for mental poverty, expressed, for example, in behavioural difficulties or low self-esteem. Neither contribute to positive experiences.

What follows are five fundamental ways in which the education system plays out – and negatively impacts on the psychology of young people:

1. Conformity: an industrial age value

    We still educate children in batches and govern the routine of their daily lives at school by ringing bells at specified intervals. All day long, young people do little but follow instructions. Sit down, take out your books, turn to page 40, stop running, solve problem number 3, stop talking, tuck in your shirt. At school, you are rewarded for doing exactly what you're told. These are the kind of industrial age values and behaviours that were really important for work in a 19th- and 20th-century factory environment. Success depended on following instructions and doing exactly what you were told, without question or deviation.

    In today's world, how far can you get by simply following instructions? The modern world employer values people who can be creative, innovative, communicate their ideas effectively, think on their feet, solve problems that have never been solved and collaborate with others. But too few of our children get the chance to develop such skills in a system that's built on industrial age values.

    You might argue that this is an overly simplistic interpretation. I suspect you can cite situations in which your own students are encouraged to collaborate, work on team projects, develop oral and tech communication skills and mastery. However, underpinning any of those activities will be the age-old requirement to do as you're told and to follow instructions to the letter. Young people today are simply learning how to regurgitate the same information we were. Why? Because it's the only way you'll pass the exam.

    The real world requires confidence to challenge, to question, to innovate and to experiment with failure. The demands upon this young generation are great. They are being tasked with solving problems created by previous generations, so the answers will not come from doing things how they've always been done.

    Think: The clichéd definition of insanity is to keep doing the same thing and expecting a different result. And yet this is the premise upon which formal education is predicated.

2. Lack of autonomy and control

    In my experience working with all ages struggling with their mental health, the key factor in a person's struggle is a sense of powerlessness and lack of control. Whilst it might be expressed as a lack of control over certain aspects of their lives, such as eating, cleaning, tidying, smoking, drinking or self-harm, this is always a symptom of the deep-seated (acquired) belief they are not in control of their own lives. Can you imagine how you would feel if you were told exactly what to do for every minute of your life? The majority of schoolchildren experience almost a complete lack of autonomy and control. Even if they seem outwardly confident, it is often a surface-level confidence demonstrated by the ability to say or do the 'right' thing according to someone else's rules or systems. Unfortunately, the common style of modern parenting, typified by fear of the unknown and stranger danger, means for many young people that their social life and 'free time' is also strictly controlled.

This level of control at school and at home is a constraint that robs too many young people of their ability to think independently and to thrive. It is not privilege or exam passes that develops self-belief and true confidence to be themselves, it is confidence in their own decision-making, confidence to risk failure and learn from it, confidence to be innovative, creative and to establish self-belief in the development of their own resources to cope with whatever life throws at them so they can live happy and fulfilling adult lives. These are the true hallmarks of a mentally wealthy individual.

Some children's lives are contained and controlled by the genuinely dangerous environment many live in where they are subjected to the control of gangs and gang culture on the streets they live in. Lacking self-belief and inner courage can make this environment even more dangerous. If you see no future exit that offers something better, you will become sucked in, no matter your ability to conform to school rules or your ability to perform well in tests.

For those unfortunate children who experience a complete lack of routine or predictability in their home environment (which also robs them of autonomy and control), it is easy to argue that the regularity and routine of school bells and regulations contribute to a sense of safety. However, there are simpler and more effective ways to provide routine and security without further stripping young people of autonomy or control.

When it comes to succeeding in any fulfilling terms in today's world, it is also the case that, if you're doing important work, then you're managing your own time, making your own decisions about what to do and when to do it. Life at school looks very different to this.

The education system is sending a dangerous message to our children that they are not in charge of their own lives. They have to follow whatever is laid down instead of taking charge and making the most of their lives. It's no wonder that our children risk becoming bored and demotivated and failing to 'achieve' the educational standards laid down for them.

Consistency of mood and attendance in staff provides adequate levels of safety and security for students, without rule-based constraints that suffocate and control. Which is why staff well-being is a lynchpin of successful students and whole-school well-being. This should extend not only to teaching staff, but also to support staff.

3. Primitive performance measurement

Most of the learning that happens in schools relies on memory retention and conformity to set guidelines. Through the curriculum, the system defines a generic set of knowledge that all children must know, and then every few months we measure how much has been retained by administering exams and tests. We know that such learning is not authentic because most of it is forgotten the day after the exam. Good teachers work hard to create deeper and more authentic learning experiences, but the system rarely rewards them for their creativity, ingenuity and passion (the very skills children *really* need). Instead, they might be admonished and advised to stick to the more traditional styles of testing and teaching and put under significant pressure to deliver against aggregated targets for passes and grades. Why? Because that's the only thing we measure and test scores are the only thing we value. This has created an extremely unhealthy culture for students, parents and teachers. Children are going through endless hours of tuition, staying up at night memorising facts that lack context and that they will very soon forget. Teachers fall out of love with the very profession they joined to make a difference and they leave. In their droves. You end up with higher rates of staff absence, staff turnover, demotivation, increased costs through recruitment and supply teaching, and the knock-on effects of children without the very continuity that would serve them well. In the long term, nobody wins.

4. Uniformity

To meet the needs of timetables, staff availability and rigid testing regimes, we have an extremely standardised system where each child must learn, and be tested on, the same thing at the same time and in pretty much the same way as everyone else. This doesn't respect the basic fact of being human, that each of us is different and uniquely skilled in our own way. There seems to be no room in the current education system for the most important questions in a child's life: 'What am I good at? What do I want to do in life? How do I fit into this world?'. The system doesn't seem to be too interested – or, rather, it's ill-equipped and out of touch with the depth and range of career options that exist for young people with nothing more than a powerful interest and desire to succeed, irrespective of formal qualification In the 20th century, you might have argued that a narrow, formal education was the exact requirement for any work of note that paid well and was well respected (reflecting 1950s values). You might also have argued that the talented people who failed in the traditional school system but succeeded beyond it were rare. You'd be right on one level – rare to have the wherewithal to overcome these failures, but not so rare that their negative experience was not shared by many. The tragedy is that, despite our obsession with measurement and data, we have no measure for how much talent or how much potential goes unrecognised in the current system.

The problem for a child who doesn't *feel* they 'fit' with the traditionally acceptable version of achievement and learning risks loss of identity and belonging which are core to their sense of psychological safety and increase that sense of cognitive dissonance. It is all too easy to believe this applies to a small minority who demonstrate behavioural issues and rule breaking and treat this as a behavioural issue which needs remedying. Those with good mental resilience will be able to recover from this apparent negation (in their eyes) of their personality and beliefs. However, it's important to understand that it's how this leads them to *feel* which is important, not how they behave. Many children will feel this and you will never know, but it will negatively impact on their mental health and future fulfilment just the same. Change the narrative.

5. Limited capacity for difference

Each of us is also different in how we learn, in how much time we take to learn something and what tools and resources work best for us. Even though the system makes provision for this in some cases, by identifying those with special educational needs (SEN) and allocating special resources or classroom assistants to support them, these are the very resources top of the list of budget cuts when money is tight. There isn't really much provision or room for differences amongst students beyond those that are diagnosed. So, if a young person is a bit slower in learning something, they might learn to consider themselves a failure when all they needed was a bit more time to catch up – or a more accessible way of learning the same information. Too often, SEN is simply a means of marginalising groups as 'different' and not in a good way. It flies in the face of professed equality and diversity.

In short, our system of education, which evolved in the industrial age, has become outmoded, outdated and ineffective. If we want to prepare our children for the modern world, if we want learning to be effective and engaging, if we want to build

Time for change

lifetime mental wealth building skills, then there's no doubt that we need to fundamentally change our system of education.

Please look beyond the idea that the only people who can succeed in the way Daniel Priestley describes (see Chapter 1) conform to the stereotypical success ladder of exam and grade passes, university attendance and degree completion. The world is changing and maybe it is for us to learn from young people, rather than the other way round. If we insist on filling their heads with the old way, the old rules, the old order, the old system, we set up a disconnect in their minds that they will try hard to resolve internally, but which cannot be resolved. So, in an effort to fit in and please either you, the teacher, or the parent, or the policymaker, they deny their own truth and mistrust their own instinct and the evidence of their eyes. Alternatively, they (rightly?) reject the lifestyle you are 'selling' and, again, because of the disconnect and trying to resolve internally (which isn't possible as the two ways of thinking cannot co-exist), they therefore reject everything you say and everything for which you stand. They become troublesome and cause problems in your classroom or further afield. Some will be fortunate enough to figure their own way through this – and they will become the new entrepreneurs. However, many will not. They will fall through the cracks – or should I say abyss – that we have created. They will, as ever, question their ability, their skill, their capacity and, most sad of all, their right to have any of the success that exists for them when they trust themselves and pursue what they know is possible. Now more than ever, the answer truthfully is that anything is possible. You are not guaranteed a life of destitution or the shop floor, weekly pay slip mediocrity because you did not get the right exam pass or grade. You will only suffer that future if you accept that the only true and valid route to career success, financial success (and implicitly happiness) is the traditional path that we followed. There is more at the end of the rainbow than this – and it is our job to help lay the bricks of the yellow brick road that gets them there.

The dissonance we create in the minds of young people by peddling these well-meant lies is the source of significant discontent, and discontent breeds anxiety or anger, both of which are key physiological indicators for future or current mental health difficulties, whether they are severe enough to be diagnosed and pathologised or whether they are just handicaps with which we live.

Any other suggested future is a lie.

Faulty goal setting and the impact on mental health

Policymakers and university academics drive us forward with old truths that no longer hold up. They overlook the bulk of findings in the very reports they commission. Why would they do that? Sadly, the truth is not seen as a vote winner for policymakers and jeopardises a funding stream for universities.

Here's a prime example:

The Augar Review, 'Post-18 Review of Education and Funding: Independent Panel Report' (published 30 May 2019; see www.gov.uk/government/publications/post-18-review-of-education-and-funding-independent-panel-report) was commissioned by Prime Minister Theresa May, yet, according to Radio 4's Analysis (The Forgotten Half), huge swathes of guidance relating to non-university pathways were as good as ignored by media and politicians alike.

Given that the review was about post-18 education, you might wonder what this has to do with secondary education – and mental health. The answer is lots. Without suitable guidance throughout the secondary years, young people will make momentous decisions about their future learning and career that can limit – or enhance – their entire economic future, their relationships and their mental fitness. Work will form a huge chunk of any person's life, which means that finding work in which you feel a sense of fulfilment, belonging, identity and value is fundamental to your long-term mental fitness. You might argue that is a valid justification for emphasising the importance of passing exams and achieving good grades. However, the impact of misguidance towards university and/ or academic performance at the expense of other, equally valid and valuable courses of education and career is profound on long-term mental fitness and mental wealth building tools. (Remember autonomy and empowerment? Belonging and identity?)

> 'There is evidence that schools still fail to tell pupils about the full range of post-18 options'
>
> *(Augar Report, May 2019).*

The following is a direct extract from the report to demonstrate how important it is for school leaders to do their own research and to embrace the changes in demand to support positive lifetime outcomes for young people leaving secondary education.

> A young person who has four or more encounters with an employer is 86 per cent less likely to be not in education, employment or training (NEET) and can earn up to 22 per cent more during their career, compared to those who did not have any such encounters.
>
> *(Augar Report, 30 May 2019).*

This short sentence, found on page 55 of the report, has huge implications. Effectively, whilst parents and teachers are persistently driving home the importance of university over alternative routes to work, young people who follow this guidance to their cost will be 22% worse off throughout their career, impacting their capacity to plan financially for the future. Financial stress can exacerbate other mental stresses and increase a sense of disempowerment (if those vital secondary years were not spent in an empowering environment, which prioritised the strengthening of personal resources of self-determination over pressure to achieve grades and passes).

The stress and anxiety associated with dissatisfaction in work and study, though recognised on a personal level, is undervalued and probably hugely underestimated in society as a factor in maintaining mental fitness or falling into mental ill health.

The report continues:

> We (also) believe that schools should be held to account for their statutory responsibility to provide IAG (Information, Advice and Guidance). We welcome the new requirement on schools (from January 2018) to allow technical education and apprenticeship providers to talk to pupils, but were disappointed to learn that there is evidence that schools still fail to tell pupils about the full range of post-18 options.
>
> *(Author parenthesis and italics. p. 55)*

Schools are so focused on outcomes that relate only to what is achieved up to the point of leaving – in other words, exam success and behaviour in school – that they are myopic around the impact on life outcomes and benefits for pupils.

Although young people may not know the reasons for this, they sense the disconnect (cognitive dissonance again). They know when they are not comfortable with traditional pathways or traditional ways of learning but, whether through well-intentioned but poorly informed information, advice and guidance (IAG), or through wilful ignorance of the facts, school policy of valuing university and academic study above other forms of learning or progress, can make them feel isolated and under-valued at a time when they are extremely vulnerable. It can increase any sense they might already have of 'not fitting in' and, in many cases, can lead to what is perceived within school as poor behaviour – or, as previously mentioned, cognitive dissonance (see p. 33).

Yet, policymakers and educators tenaciously hang onto their old model of the world. It's been around – and seemed valid – for so long, it seems to be regarded as an immutable truth, rather than a mindset that could be shifted, a way of thinking and behaving that could be changed. In this, we see one of the key elements of a fixed mindset[3] within the very fabric of education and its institutions. In my view, this is one of the key reasons attempts to apply growth mindset teaching to improve performance has been reported to fail in the United Kingdom; and why original research outcomes can't be replicated.[4]

The negative mental health impact of achieving grades

If you were to rely on the evidence of Twitter feeds and staff room chat, you would be led to believe that the pressure to focus on achieving predicted grades comes exclusively from policymakers and Ofsted. Yet, *Schools Week* reported that Anna Spielman, Ofsted's chief inspector at the time of writing, spoke at a National Governance Association Conference in June 2019 and told the conference that

> "predicting grades and comparing them against actual outcomes can have a "very, very powerful effect on making all the school conversation about how the target numbers are going to be achieved rather than about making sure children have the best possible education.

Spielman also warned schools against collecting internal data in a way that 'puts undue pressure on teachers' time' and said that if a school's data collection system is 'disproportionate or inefficient or unsustainable for staff' then Ofsted will reflect this in their inspection report 'and could well grade the school less than good'[5].

Whilst it can be heartening to hear policymakers speak out in this way, acting on fine words is a completely different story. Like the vast ship that it is, the system of secondary education and its associated 'belief systems' turns slowly.

The pressure is felt by students and teachers alike, each feeling a sense of failure for not achieving what they are, arguably, supposed to achieve (according to a board of governors, trustees or you, the head teacher and your senior leadership team), and each experiencing additional pressure from parents. If a student doesn't achieve predicted grades, then they are led to believe they aren't achieving their potential. Yet, there are so many erroneous and random assumptions and inferences tied up in this.

Firstly, human potential is bigger than an exam grade. Secondly, although we have a fixed age for going through formal education, this does not signify a lack of future

Time for change

opportunity throughout life to achieve on all kinds of levels that relate to potential. Thirdly, if the skill or talent that a young person is strongest in is not something valued or, possibly more importantly, tested in your school, then they may internalise that lack of value as a lack of self-worth. Fourthly, predicting grades (crystal ball, anyone?) is highly subjective, skewed as much towards behaviour and attendance as performance (even if this is unconscious bias, it is still bias). Whilst a King's College research study shows there is accuracy in those predictions,[6] which has made it acceptable – and popular – for exam grades under Covid restrictions to be determined by teachers instead of examination, there exists the problematic power of suggestion and self-fulfilling prophecy, also known as the Pygmalion Effect.[7] Put simply, if a teacher thinks a student will do well, it is likely they will – and vice versa (even if the teacher's expectation bears no relation to the grade the student is capable of). This can be highly detrimental and potentially harmful to a young person's current self-belief and entire future expectations of themselves.

The Pygmalion Effect

The work of Rosenthal and Jacobsen (1968), among others, shows that teacher expectations influence student performance. Positive expectations influence performance positively, and negative expectations influence performance negatively. Rosenthal and Jacobson originally described the phenomenon as the Pygmalion Effect.

'When we expect certain behaviors of others, we are likely to act in ways that make the expected behavior more likely to occur'

(Rosenthal and Babad, 1985).

In terms of teaching, faculty who gripe about students establish a climate of failure, but faculty who value their students' abilities create a climate of success.[8]

There's other mental health risks too. High performers, for example, on learning of their predicted grades may push themselves even harder to achieve, disregarding any internal warning systems for maintaining positive mental fitness. They may distance themselves from social engagement (too tired and too busy) and sport or leisure activity (too tired and too busy). Alternatively, they push on with extra-curricular activity *and* pile on the extra home study, pushing themselves to stay up late to complete assignments and achieve those all too important grades. Each of these factors impairs their emotional well-being and mental health. They can become sleep deprived, impacting on performance (and leading them to drive themselves harder to compensate). They may feel a sense of (unjustified) guilt if they don't believe they are working hard enough and this can lead to shame expressed as 'I am not good enough'. None of which expands the mental wealth building skill. It's easy to write this off as short-term pressure, that we must all come to experience in life – and be resilient enough to come out the other side mentally unscathed. This, I suspect, is where much of the mythology and misunderstanding around resilience – and the younger generation's alleged lack of it – stems. It is true that occasional acute stimulation of our parasympathetic nervous system, which triggers our fight, flight or freeze response to release adrenaline and cortisol into the bloodstream will desensitise us to stress (which is why a regime of cold water swimming or cold showers is hugely beneficial for anyone suffering with stress or anxiety). However, chronic

23

Time for change

stress has a completely opposite effect. It diminishes our resistance to stress and weakens our immune system, making us at greater risk of impaired physical *and* mental health.

Relentless testing and measurement can put young people under undue pressure with little respite. So, the very measures you might think are building their resilience are, in greater likelihood, diminishing it.

It is not the examinations and tests per se that create the pressure. It is the expectation of teachers and head teachers to perform in a certain way and at a certain level that is the problem. As a leader, you can break this pattern in a heartbeat. General Certificates of Secondary Education (GCSEs) and A-levels are intended as a measure of a young person's learning in a specific subject area. They – and their parents – expect that. Standard assessment tests (SATS) and other tests, on the other hand, are really a measure of your performance as a school. Projecting your organisational performance pressure onto students is unfair and unnecessary, and smacks of weak leadership. Without projected teacher expectation, such tests should be part of a normal day, like an average classroom test of subject learning.

Even though there may be short-term performance pay-offs in grades (confirming those 'crystal ball' predictions), over time the excess stress brought on by fewer opportunities to relax and 'chill' activates the fear system in the brain, which increases anxiety and makes it harder to focus. This impairs learning, driving a negative cycle of worry impacting performance and impacting anxiety. It's a potent cocktail, strongly increasing the likelihood of some future manifestation of mental ill health. If not creating a visible impact during the secondary years, then it can almost certainly cause knock-on problems in sixth form or university when internal (and external) pressures increase.

> Young people today are anxious. We know that. They're showing up at college with unprecedented levels of mental health diagnoses. They're reluctant to detach from their parents. They're afraid (understandably) for the future of the planet, as well as their own futures. They can also, I've noticed, be afraid of their own thoughts. I've often heard them say they're afraid to say out loud what they really think, as if their thoughts are embarrassing involuntary reflexes they're compelled to hide.[9]

At the other end of the spectrum, young people who are told their predicted grades are poor can adopt an 'identity' of failure, a mindset of inadequacy and poor self-worth that says, why bother? They can either rebel or engage in disruptive behaviour (they don't fit your version of what's expected, so why not?) or they can simply give up, making little or no effort in subjects they are never going to do well in because you said so. Feeling bad about yourself, when you sense you aren't valued as highly as others, is not good for mental fitness. Again, it can drive a downward spiral of stress and negativity, leading to behavioural problems and poor mental health. If they're lucky enough to have adequate resilience and a 'growth mindset' (Carol Dweck), they can respond to feedback, setbacks and criticism with curiosity and use poor grades as opportunities to learn more and bounce back stronger.

The trouble is, if your school doesn't teach students resilience or provide them with tools for building mental wealth and self-worth, those well-intentioned grade predictions will have no positive outcomes and, probably, a heap of negative ones.

Why then do we subject young people to a set of beliefs that suggests achievement of good grades at school is their only chance to make anything of themselves, that there will be no other chance and that failure to meet the demands and targets set out for them now, will mean failure for the rest of their lives?

It isn't true and it can be seriously detrimental to their mental fitness.

This harks back to 20th-century life, a time when education was a golden, once in a lifetime opportunity, a gateway to professions and a more comfortable life, one in which you might move up through the socio-economic strata. Adult education, personal development and a plethora of materials and on and offline opportunities for learning did not exist. Which is not to say that I'm overlooking the very real truth that, if people fail to engage with learning during the school years, their likelihood and potential for re-engaging later in life can seem to be restricted by opportunity and funding. Yet, I would suggest this: part of the reason why career change or post-18 learning becomes so hard for those who didn't engage during secondary education is because of the values and beliefs we inculcate during that education. In other words, if we teach them that this is their *only* opportunity, that they have failed if they don't achieve the right grades, or behave in suitably conforming ways, then we make it a self-fulfilling prophecy. We are setting them up to fail if they don't do as we say.

Performance gap and mental health

We know that the performance gap is growing, rather than shrinking, and there are increasing numbers of disadvantaged young people in our communities. There are also many teachers and leaders, much like you, who are dedicated to wanting to change this. Some do so because they come from less advantaged backgrounds themselves. Others do so simply because they care. The reason most teachers go into teaching is to make a difference and to share a passion for their subject or simply for learning. Despite this, little changes for the children who come from less advantaged backgrounds. The projections for their life outcomes are not good.

A study by the Education Policy Institute think tank in 2019, showed that the gap which had been narrowing since 2011, actually widened in 2018 and that 'persistently disadvantaged students were almost 2 years behind their peers by the time they finish GCSEs'.[10] Looked after children fare even worse. Low attainment is matched by low personal expectation and low self-esteem. Low self-esteem is a clear sign of mental poverty.

Although it's material poverty that gets measured, it's rare, in the West, for material poverty to go unmatched by mental poverty. If you don't believe life holds much possibility for you, whatever you do, you are already at risk of anxiety, depression and anger – all core elements within the mental poverty spectrum. Although teachers can – and do – make a huge difference to some children, it is rarely by following the standard curriculum or by working within the confines of their daily timetable. Exceptional outcomes come about as a result of exceptional teaching, demonstrated by dedication, extra hours and enormous amounts of energy and sensitivity to the individual. No amount of generic 'positive thinking' can overcome the evidence all around a young person. If their friends, families and the people on their street live lives of quiet desperation with no jobs, low-paid, low-skilled jobs or crime and addiction, then no amount of blathering on about grades and effort will make much of a dent in their expectation of what they think is achievable for them. Theirs is not just a performance or wealth issue, it is an enormous mental fitness issue.

The tragedy is that, despite much fanfare and political posturing, and despite specific funding measures, there has been little improvement in closing the class and

Time for change

performance gap since the 1970s when I was at school. In fact, a report published in August 2019 by the Education Policy Institute stated that the closing of any gap had slowed to a standstill:

> *"For the most persistently disadvantaged pupils the gap has narrowed at primary level but widened at secondary level. This means that these pupils – the very worst-off – are almost two years (22.6 months) behind all other pupils by the time they finish their GCSEs....*
>
> *...Over recent years, there has been a dramatic slowing down in the closure of the disadvantage gap to the extent that the five year rolling average now suggests that it would take 560 years to close the gap. However, the most recent data shows an increase in the gap in 2018 suggesting there is a real risk that we could be at a turning point and that we could soon enter a period where the gap starts to widen."*[11]

PERFORMANCE GAP AND MENTAL ILL HEALTH

(Mental health) Disorders were more common among children living in lower income households and children whose parents were in receipt of low-income benefits. Disorders were also more likely among children who had experienced challenging life situations, such as their parents separating or having financial difficulties.

(Source: www.mentalhealth.org.uk/blog/what-new
-statistics-show-about-childrens-mental-health)

I'd like to significantly reduce that, wouldn't you?

Apart from anything else, the persistent performance gap can also contribute to a weakened ability to achieve mental fitness amongst those disadvantaged children. Which is not to say that mental ill health is the sole domain of the economically disadvantaged children in your school. Quite the contrary. Again, relating this to physical fitness, whilst a physical disability does not automatically mean you cannot achieve physical fitness, it might mean your capacity to achieve that fitness is limited by the expectations of those around you.

Those expectations can be altered and enhanced by greater inclusivity, which provides a sense of belonging. In turn, this helps affirm identity and build self-belief. These are the foundation stones of good mental health for the long term and it's true that every school strives for this. However, few of them excel.

The adolescent desire to belong drives much of their tribal behaviour and they are highly sensitive to subtle – and not so subtle – symbols of exclusion (such as uniform requirements, strict behavioural conformity, language mastery and, of course, the backgrounds of their own teachers, governors and other support staff).

Schools demand conformity and compliance. A demand for conformity and compliance breeds homogeneity. This means that those who do not conform or are not compliant become outsiders, excluded. So there is no coincidence that exclusions are rife. The entire school system is exactly that – excluding and exclusive. If you fit, you stand a chance, but too many young people are square pegs being forced into round holes. For inclusivity to be genuine, it needs to be reflected within every strata of the school. Which means from the governors down.

Your role as a pioneer

Only you can decide how to empower yourself, your staff and your students, and to make shifts in your own thinking and practices within your own school. However, it is insufficient to claim disempowerment, to claim you are nothing more than a cog in a system that is bigger than you. Thinking of the Industrial Revolution analogy, it might have served short-term goals for a factory manager to sacrifice the well-being of factory workers in the interests of factory owner profit, to discount the 'churn' of employees falling sick and unable to work because of a ready supply of replacements, but systemic change requires pioneers. You have just such an opportunity.

Throughout the pages of this book, I provide insights into the hidden mental health costs of routine decision-making, employment practice, performance targets and measurement, school rules and regulations. It would, however, remain easy to walk away from the challenges presented by powerful mental health leadership. No one would blame you (though your conscience might quietly gnaw away at you, further damaging your own mental fitness). Please be assured, therefore, that I also provide ways for you to make extraordinarily simple shifts in your own thinking and behaviour that have a powerful domino effect on everyone around you.

When the biggest transformations occur at an individual level (and they do), it is impossible for those changes not to have a knock-on effect on everyone in the surrounding environment. So, simply making a change for yourself will be a huge step forwards in making a change for everyone. Start small. Allow change to happen. Watch it gather momentum.

When best efforts aren't enough

I know that many committed teachers are passionate and work incredibly hard to be inclusive and creative about the content they deliver, encouraging all young people to collaborate in acquiring the learning that they need. However, they can't change the system of education alone. Without enough bold leaders and head teachers, I think it's no surprise that so many leave the profession. It's also no coincidence that some of the most successful entrepreneurs I know in the coaching space are ex-teachers.

There's something fundamentally flawed about traditional 'teaching' when it's predicated on imparting knowledge, facts, concepts or understanding to another person.

When you work hard to find different ways to communicate information to make it easier for people to grasp and remember, it's both exhausting for you, as the teacher, and difficult for the learner. In school, if you can't learn something easily, you don't pass exams or get the grades and you can feel a sense of failure, a lack of worth. That's inbuilt into the system. It may have nothing to do with intelligence, commitment, hard work or willingness. But it can crush your confidence and self-esteem if you don't achieve according to the measures of success laid down by others.

The best coaches and therapists know that the clients who make the most successful transition from problems to solutions are not those to whom you give the answer. They are those who you enable to find the answer for themselves. Your job as educators is

Time for change

to inspire someone to learn and explore and discover and take risks with that learning. This style of teaching is empowering, enabling and supportive of mental wealth building. The more you encourage it, the greater the students' confidence becomes and the more frequently they experience a sense of achievement – even in the 'failures'. You know that. Yet, every school leader who puts exam passes and grades ahead of mental wealth building is compromising the long-term success and self-esteem of students. You are sacrificing the type of learning that leads to fully rounded human beings, equipped to succeed on their terms, not yours. And even if it were only about commercial success – in finding a 'good job' or building a sustainable business – the same rules would apply.

Employers want creative, innovative (and yes, literate and numerate) employees. Employees want to be able to manage diverse career portfolios. The long-term career has become a thing of rarity. Society wants employers who know how to work sustainably within that society, contributing solutions, rather than creating problems. Young people who are afraid to fail and are taught the old way that says racking up qualifications is the way to security and success risk failing on every level. They risk good relationships, fulfilling careers and may sacrifice the opportunities presented by lifetime learning. Success – or the sense of it – is personal. Lack of it sets up self-doubt, which precedes poor decision-making, which results in lives less worth living.

This is what mental wealth building is about. You are not fixing broken people. You are enabling capable people. There exists a world of difference in the thinking underpinning this sentence, but only a series of small shifts in the behaviours that you can implement that will transform the lives of many for the better. A mentally poor life is no fun, no matter how much money or external success you accrue. None of us is immune to mental poverty, but we could all acquire greater mental wealth building skills.

There are many examples I could cite that would confirm the truth of that statement, but I'll cite just one. Michael Phelps. Michael Phelps is, to date, the most successful swimmer ever and an 18 times gold medal–winning Olympian in multiple swimming events. Yet, there was a time when he felt like the weakest man on the planet and questioned if he wanted to go on living. Externally validated success does not equal happiness or mental fitness. It most certainly is not equivalent to internally validated success or self-esteem, which is core to building mental wealth.

> *Think: Understanding the difference between teaching someone about mental fitness and enabling them to trust their own choices and decisions that lead to mental fitness is a bit like the difference between force-feeding someone something that they might well enjoy, but didn't ask for right now, versus simply giving them access to the kitchen and resources that help them know what to do when they are ready.*

This is critically important when it comes to mental fitness, because when we feel empowered to make choices, even wrong ones, we learn to exercise autonomy.

Too often, education doesn't encourage young people to trust their own desires or beliefs, or to follow up on their interests if they don't align with those of the school. Instead, they are strongly advised on what is or isn't sensible (especially when it comes to career and education choices), as if a teacher's life experience is so wide and all-encompassing that they know all the answers themselves. We know that isn't true and yet we often act as if it is.

Mental health and mental wealth building cannot be isolated and compartmentalised like geography, French or history. It is something we live with and experience in every waking and non-waking moment. We take it with us wherever we go, whatever we are doing, whoever we are with. It has a touchpoint in every single aspect of our lives. It impacts on how you feel about yourself, your life and whether you have confidence and resilience to move forwards. As human beings, we cannot isolate ourselves from the world around us. As teachers and leaders, you cannot isolate yourselves or your students from the environment they live in. Which means you can't just delegate or apply a quick fix or isolated solution. You need to apply all-encompassing changes to the way you think about your own mental health, in order to enable changes in the way your staff and pupils think about theirs. Thoughts lead to beliefs. Beliefs lead to actions. And it starts with you.

It is within your control as a leader to alter the school environment (for environment, read culture) as best you can to improve someone's chances of building those skills of resilience beyond the school gates, but before you do that, you need to invest some time in exploring what the hell resilience really is, rather than the surface-level, populist notion that it has something to do with grit, stiff upper lip, push on through the pain or put up and shut up.

Your leadership skills allow you to create and foster an environment in which the mental fitness of the teaching staff, the support staff and the students is the priority. As each person feels more empowered to grow, starting with you, they start to feel better about themselves. In so doing, they feel more courageous to take the risks that are required to grow as capable, resourceful human beings. They discover strength to cope with the kind of setbacks that are a normal part of living. These are the skills required of a thriving human being in the 21st century. Above and beyond any grades attained or numbers of exam passes, these are the skills that enable young people to thrive in this extraordinary world that changes day by day, moment by moment. It gives them the personal resources to hit the ground running when they leave your school gates for the last time. It gives them a head start on their own journey through life. And isn't that the point?

Notes

1 Michael Peterson, 2009, WholeSchooling.net, www.wholeschooling.net/WS/WSPrncples/WS%200%20purpose%20schls.html.
2 Seth Godin: 'The sole intention of the education system was to train people to be willing to work in a factory'. Ken Robinson: 'Education is modelled in the interests of the industrial age and in the image of it'. Source: https://martinbrown3.medium.com/is-the-school-education-system-outdated-and-why-2c0fd4db9391.
3 Source: Carol Dweck, *Mindset: Changing the Way You Think to Fulfil Your Potential*, 2012, Robinson.
4 Source: https://unherd.com/2019/08/the-myth-of-the-growth-mindset/.
5 https://schoolsweek.co.uk/spielman-schools-should-put-less-faith-in-predicted-grades/
6 Source: www.kcl.ac.uk/news/teachers-predict-pupil-success-just-as-well-as-exam-scores.
7 Source: www.duq.edu/about/centers-and-institutes/center-for-teaching-excellence/teaching-and-learning-at-duquesne/pygmalion.
8 See more at www.duq.edu/about/centers-and-institutes/center-for-teaching-excellence/teaching-and-learning-at-duquesne/pygmalion.
9 Meghan Daum, Advice for Millennials: The Case for Spacing Out, May 2019, Medium.
10 Source: Guardian Online, 30 July 2019, Sally Weale, www.theguardian.com/education/2019/jul/30/attainment-gap-widens-disadvantaged-gcse-pupils-study.
11 Source: www.bbc.co.uk/news/education-49150993.

Chapter 3

Doing your best?

In the words of Seth Godin, 'This isn't a prescription. It's not a manual. It's a series of provocations, ones that might resonate and that I hope will provoke conversation'[1]

The best and quickest way to change or influence another person's behaviour is to change your own.

First and foremost, this means putting your own personal mental health house in order. If you are personally experiencing any of the following (to name a common few) – stress, overwhelm, irritability, insomnia, fatigue, all-or-nothing thinking, self-doubt, lows or anxious feelings – you are in no position to be leading or supporting others in strengthening their own personal resources and developing powerful systems for positive changes in mental health and well-being.

Mental ill health and mental poverty do not spontaneously occur. They are the result of a layering of events, situations and adverse experiences. It is why you need to critically evaluate the risk and potential impact of *every* aspect of school organisation, not just discrete parts of it. It's also vital to incorporate an assessment of how the world outside impacts on your staff and students, and how what you do within the confines of the school gates affects them on the world outside. You might think you do this and that it is patronising to suggest you don't. However, it is all too easy to exist inside the 'bubble' of education. When the majority of your professional (and often social) contact time is with others in the 'bubble', impartiality and objectivity become almost impossible to achieve without the perspective of people outside looking in.

In some cases, I've had head teachers refuse to acknowledge that any of this is their problem at all, that it is a health issue for healthcare providers, that the fact that they have an onsite counsellor, a quiet room and a (partial) personal, social and health education (PSHE) programme, with occasional assemblies or mental health weeks is enough. In fact, they refuse to entertain more, because they perceive it is a cost they are unwilling or unable to commit funds to or they claim their job is merely to educate (aka, get the numbers of desired General Certificate in Secondary Education [GCSE] passes and grades).

It's understandable. Your school may have invested in specially trained counsellors, mentors or therapists to support children showing signs of difficulty, yet it can seem that the more resources that get thrown at the problem, the bigger the problem gets.

DOI: 10.4324/9780429353420-3

Doing your best?

In their own words

Anonymous Year 10

Nobody understands what I'm going through. They tell me I should stay off social media because none of it's real. It's hard though. I'm not stupid, but I'm so lonely and scared. Every time I walk down my street. I'm scared that I might be the next person to be in the wrong place at the wrong time. And I'm scared of some of the comments and messages I get too. Some people say bad things about me. I can't tell my teachers or Mum and Dad – even though they say I should. They don't really get it. If I tell them it will just get worse.

But some of those other people on social media give me hope. Maybe if I did buy those things they recommend, eat like them, exercise like them or look like them, I might be happier. If I don't believe in the dream, what else is there?

I have to have something to believe in.

My older sister thinks I'm gullible comparing myself to someone else's so-called perfect life. If I ate healthier, I bet people would like me more though.

Mum tells me to get off the phone and see what's around me, to communicate in person, to go out more. But being home feels safer – and my friends are all on social media too. If I'm not online too, I might miss out. It is addictive though. When I go to bed, I don't sleep for hours. My friends are messaging and posting. I need to know who's saying or doing what. Sometimes I make new friends here too even though they sometimes get me to do things I don't think I should be doing. Everyone else is though, aren't they?

I'm tired most days. And there are some people who say bad things about me and send me nasty messages. They pick on me at the school bus stop and on the way to school too. I daren't tell anyone. It will only get worse. Sometimes I wonder what it would be like if I never went to school again. Sometimes I even wonder what it would be like if I never woke up again.

Mental health: not your problem?

Studies carried out by National Health Service (NHS) Digital confirm that there is definitely an upward trend in mental ill health amongst young people (Mental Health of Children and Young People in England, 2020: Wave 1 follow up to the 2017 survey[2]). So, by the time the current school generation is in their thirties this increase will play out in the workplace. Why? Because, historically, adult mental health problems begin in childhood.

It is, in my view, no longer acceptable (if it ever was) to regard mental ill health as a health sector problem and therefore wash our hands of any role in the creation or resolution of such problems, within any sector of society, least of all within education.

I get it. You see your own organisational and personal workload burgeoning. In order to gain some greater sense of control, you focus your attention on core school responsibilities. Shifting mental health out of your line of vision makes perfect sense. Lack of planning and resources in the health sector shouldn't be your problem.

On a personal level, you take the emotional well-being of students very seriously. However, when the core focus of school performance is numbers on roll and exam grades and passes, you will, by default, choose policies and procedures that can work to the detriment of that emotional well-being and unintentionally contribute to the severity of pupil and staff mental ill health.

A couple of decades ago, ignorance might have been a form of defence, but not now. It's analogous with the impact of passive smoking. For a long time, no one knew how dangerous it was. Now we do. And so smoking is banned in all public spaces – and most smokers wouldn't dream of subjecting other people to their habit, even in their own home.

You are not alone as a head teacher or mental health lead if you find mental health an enticing, but thorny topic. It's high profile. It's in the news daily. It makes Twitter comments go viral and it gets under the skin of teachers and head teachers alike – for good or for bad.

Some, like you, care passionately about making a positive change. Yet, few know precisely what to do about it.

Maybe you've implemented mental health weeks, invited specialist speakers on mental health topics to speak at assemblies or to run PSHE classes. Many schools – and yours may be one of them – have a range of highly positive initiatives, including student mental health ambassadors, motivational role models delivering speeches, quotes on display around the school, mental health help and information displayed prominently.

Some even go so far as to say that they are already implementing proven strategies such as positive psychology and growth mindset. This is a huge leap in the right direction. However, from what I hear and see, a lot of these solutions are DIY adaptations, based on reading a couple of articles, attending a couple of conferences or simply fuelled by the laudable and well-intentioned passion of an individual teacher.

The trouble with data

The trouble is that, even if you're the head teacher, policymaking often seems to sit outside your domain of control. The 'powers that be' may seem to demand you focus on data and data reporting. You're not seen as doing your job properly if you fail to focus on data. Data feels safer, feels predictable, controllable, is certainly measurable – and we're all taught that goals need to be smart. Specific, measurable, attainable, realistic, timely. And well-being can't be accurately measured against any of those criteria. So you get lost in the data – and mire your team in data too.

It can seem like you have perfectly good justification for doing so, because:

- you can't accurately measure or even define well-being
- if you can't measure or define it, you certainly can't set a goal for it
- if you can't set a goal for it, you can't achieve it

All of which seems to provide the perfect get-out clause that means you carry on as you were. Except you wouldn't have picked up this book if that's what you thought.

A simple one-step solution

I'll let you into a secret that is so incredibly simple you might think I'm being facetious, fatuous even. It is this:

Doing your best?

Set the core policy and mission for your school as positive well-being

Yes, that's it. If you embed this one fundamental change within the governance of your school and stick to it like nothing else matters (because it doesn't), everything else will improve. Recruitment and retention of staff, student and staff absenteeism, student behaviour, student and staff performance, grades and pass rates, overall school culture.

CHANGE YOUR CORE POLICY AND MISSION?

If inspiration were needed to keep you reading, to confirm that this is not some outlandish and unworkable, faddish new plan to burden you with, you may be grateful to discover that the New Zealand government has taken the bold step of putting mental fitness at the heart of policy.

They have become one of the first governments in the world to design their budget, not around monetary aims, but around well-being aims. (Maybe it's one reason they've managed the Covid-19 pandemic better than most.)[3]

It won't mean you never get challenges or problems or face obstacles along the way, but it will provide the core navigational tool for your school and the education business you're in. It will inform every decision you're tasked with making and guide you towards best practice without feeling like you have to constantly learn and reinvent what you do and how you do it. It will change any sense of being rudderless or controlled by data, yet it can, ironically, contribute to improving the very data that's getting in the way.

What am I basing this recommendation on? Am I divorced from the harsh reality of daily life, wearing rose-tinted spectacles, watching you all in the gladiator arena of education and pontificating with fluffy hippie feel-good theories? I'd get it if you thought that, especially when you read the next two sentences. **Your perception of obstacles, limitations and possibility are structures of your own thinking. Your reality is what you create.**

If you suspend judgement for a while, you will open yourself up to the potential for enabling big change. That change might just be far greater than you've allowed yourself to think possible till now. You might just be on the brink of a monumental shift within the lives of all those you impact, directly or indirectly.

Practise what you preach

Isn't what you've just read what you ask your students to believe? Or do you tell them that they may as well accept the hand they've been dealt, the lot they've been given and just knuckle down and get on with it, without argument, challenge or ambition? I don't think so.

Consider this too. When it comes to your family and your personal life, what is your number one policy for living, which guides every action you take, every decision you make and every interaction you have? Is it (a) finances and performance data or (b) mental well-being?

Sure, you care that you are making enough money to pay the bills and put a roof over your head, but what matters most to you? What really guides every decision about where

Doing your best?

you live, which schools you send your children to, what activities you – or they – engage in, what friends you – or they – have? I suspect it's mental well-being. You don't have a unifying measure for it, but it does inform and guide your decisions, without question. It provides a moral compass for what is right, fair, compassionate, just, empowering, enabling. So, every financial or data-driven decision that falls from it is guided first by mental well-being.

The first unspoken question underpinning each decision is, 'will I/we be better off (mentally/emotionally) for doing this?'.

Is it failsafe? No. Of course not. Does it get you closer to collective mental well-being than financially motivated decisions alone? Yes, probably. Does it hinder you from high achievement or good financial performance? Absolutely not.

Making that one change in thinking, using mental well-being as a benchmark for policymaking, strategic planning, tactical goal setting and day-to-day decision-making will, in my opinion, transform the way you run your school. It will also transform the lives of those in it and connected with it.

Implementing it requires honest introspection, suspending judgement, and an open mind. However, I suspect there's still that nagging doubt, that sceptic, that cynical inner demon, who believes it isn't as simple as that. So, let's visit another perspective. Let's attempt a review of the problems as they (seem to) stand.

Leadership

> Leadership requires us to look in the mirror and to clear out as much of our inner baggage as possible, so that we don't project it on to others. With leadership comes responsibility for the well-being and choices of others.[4]

Great leadership sets a more authentic example of what is permissible and desirable amongst your staff and students. It makes you more of a leader people willingly follow, rather than simply a figurehead people are compelled by status or rank to follow. Brave and powerful leadership, according to Brene Brown, requires an admission of vulnerability. Without that ownership and expression of your vulnerability, you become weaker and disempowered.

Here are the 10 behaviours and cultural issues that her research amongst senior leaders identified as 'getting in our way' in organisations across the world:

1. We avoid tough conversations, including giving honest, productive feedback… Whatever the reason, there was saturation across the data that the consequence is a lack of clarity, diminishing trust and engagement, and an increase in problematic behavior, including passive-aggressive behaviour, talking behind people's backs, pervasive back channel communication (or 'the meeting after the meeting'), gossip and the 'dirty yes' (when I say yes to your face and then no behind your back).
2. Rather than spending a reasonable amount of time proactively acknowledging and addressing the fears and feelings that show up during change and upheaval, we spend an unreasonable amount of time managing problematic behaviours.
3. Diminishing trust caused by a lack of connection and empathy.
4. Not enough people are taking smart risks or creating and sharing bold ideas to meet changing demands and the insatiable need for innovation. When people are afraid of being put down or ridiculed for trying something and failing, or even for putting forward a radical new idea, the best you can expect is status quo and groupthink.

35

Doing your best?

5. We get stuck and defined by setbacks, disappointments, and failures, so instead of spending resources on clean-up to ensure that consumers, stakeholders or internal processes are made whole, we are spending too much time and energy reassuring team members who are questioning their contribution and value.
6. Too much shame and blame, not enough accountability and learning.
7. People are opting out of vital conversations about diversity and inclusivity because they fear looking wrong, saying something wrong, or being wrong. Choosing our own comfort over hard conversations is the epitome of privilege, and it corrodes trust and moves us away from meaningful and lasting change.
8. When something goes wrong, individuals and teams are rushing into ineffective or unsustainable solutions rather than staying with problem identification and solving. When we fix the wrong thing for the wrong reason, the same problems continue to surface. It's costly and demoralizing.
9. Organizational values are gauzy and assessed in terms of aspirations rather than actual behaviours that can be taught, measured and evaluated.
10. Perfectionism and fear are keeping people from learning and growing.

(Extract from Dare to Lead, Brene Brown, 2018, Vermilion)

Does any of this sound all too familiar in your own school?

Responding to a moving landscape

It's hard to predict and plan when education policies change from year to year and with almost every change of minister in government. So, it can be a frustrating experience keeping on top of exactly what's expected. You need to ensure a raft of policies comply with statutory requirements, as well as complying with what seems to be the more fluid and sometimes unpredictable demands of individual inspectors. Add in to the mix that many parents base their children's school choices on (often unfairly) biased school reviews and public rankings and it can be hard to avoid knee-jerk responses as a head teacher. After all, those student numbers drive the income of the school, so there may be additional pressure from governors, trustees and academy boards. If you've not sufficiently honed your own mental wealth building skill (and why would you, if it's never been front of mind or you've not experienced any diagnosed mental ill health issues in the past?), this layering of pressure increases your own stress and can lead to background anxiety, even if you're unaware of it. Tell-tale signs include poor quality of sleep, increased irritability or intolerance, lapses in concentration or focus and low mood. The clearest signs are when you find yourself expecting the worst, or fretting about the past too often.

Anxious leadership can mean you interpret an inspection visit almost as a new army recruit would anticipate uniform or equipment inspection. You demand that staff and students be on their best behaviour, entreating them to present a polished veneer, and to remain vigilant of any negative or less than perfect events on the day (or in the data). In short, you foster a climate of anxiety in staff and students in your efforts to control an outcome that will reflect the school, staff and pupils in the best possible light. This approach exerts pressure equivalent to extreme cramming in exam conditions, with little emphasis on learning, or understanding as a journey to be embarked on through the year. It quite closely resembles the exact same stress and pressure felt by students as they approach their own major exams. The culture exemplified by this kind of approach to Ofsted inspections is toxic, and it is infectious, cascading tension throughout the school.

Doing your best?

The unified demand of teachers, leaders and unions is to change Ofsted and its requirements in the belief that this is the biggest source of overwhelm, overload and excessive performance monitoring in school. There's nothing intrinsically wrong in that demand. There is always plenty of room for improvement. Yet, for any changes to result in a positive force for change that pupils and staff will benefit from, the school leadership response also has to change significantly.

You may feel that too much of your time is already taken up with budget management and use this as an excuse to duck the mental health leadership mantle, delegating it to another staff member. However, if you are to be the kind of bold leader who is driven, first and foremost, by the need to serve young people well, your fundamental responsibility is to put their well-being ahead of any administrative directive. Your primary role is to serve the immediate and long-term interests of students so that they may flourish and make a positive contribution to society. If it isn't, you may be in the wrong job.

Changing outcomes

It is not what happens to us that determines future outcomes, it is how we perceive what happens to us. You may have to follow certain rules and standards, but this should never be an excuse to remain silent, to give up on your own aspirations, or acquiesce to a way of working that is detrimental to staff and students to whom you have a real duty of care. Do not allow other people's priorities to jaundice your sense of what is right, or to be the reason for not achieving what you want to achieve for your school, for your students and for yourself.

You probably would teach your students the exact same thing. You would tell them that they don't have to be moulded by, or victim to, their environment if it doesn't serve them well. You would encourage them to be bold, be courageous, to commit to the work that will get them the outcomes they want and deserve. Yet, there is no point sharing this kind of thinking with your pupils if you are not willing to embrace it and act on it yourself. To drop into a (valid) cliché for a moment, there needs to be a little less chalk and talk and a lot more walk the walk. People young and old respond far better to leadership by example (do as I do) – than leadership by slavish rules and demands (do as I say).

Fixing broken people vs. enabling resilient people

Just because you are not ill, does not mean you are fit. As a society, whilst we fully understand that being physically free of illness does not mean we are physically fit, we have more limited understanding when it comes to mental well-being. We make the assumption that if we are not mentally ill, then we must be mentally well.

Most people's thinking and behaviour around mental health have mental *ill* health as the starting point. Which means we start with trying to figure out what's wrong within an individual or targeted group, and devote resources and thinking to ways we can fix or manage the 'problem'.

Less attention is paid to how we might prevent problems and come up with long-term, sustainable strategies that teach *all* people how to improve mental health for the long term. This conforms to the traditional model of medicine and clinical practice, which is, to identify what's wrong, name it and then devote attention to how to fix it. It applies equally to broken legs, weak hearts, cancer and all things physical.

Doing your best?

Over the last few decades, exponentially increasing demand for clinical help based on this model has resulted in a shortage of treatment resources. Medicine has slowly come round to the idea that the only way to stem the tide of worsening physical health in large swathes of the population (and to better manage stretched resources) is to foster a culture of prevention. So, nowadays, you're as likely to be prescribed a book to read or an exercise class to attend as you are a drug or a stay in hospital.

Although we might be encouraged to exercise and eat well, the focus of the NHS remains predominantly about treating and managing, it is the last line of defence for government policy that omits prevention from its planning and goal setting, or pays lip service to it. Why? Because prevention is long term. Politics is short term (see inset on box ticking).

Professional mental health thinking, despite an even greater shortage of resources, also continues to focus most of its attention on diagnosing and treating – and although some practical measures are now acknowledged as effective and taught (such as meditation and mindfulness), little time or effort is invested to educate society on how to build a stock of mental wealth that will help them remain mentally well under all kinds of circumstances.

Mental wealth building

I use the analogy of wealth where others might use the term resilience. In my view, consideration of your stock of mental wealth relates well to the spectrum of economic prosperity, where you might be anywhere on a continuum between destitution and extraordinary wealth. Just because you are not poor, does not mean you are rich.

When it comes to your financial wealth, you might be well advised to save and invest for the future to offset both planned and unplanned events. From time to time, you might need to dip into those savings to help you through the tough times. However, as soon as you are able, you need to return to saving and investing, in order to replenish your depleted resources. In an ideal world, you maintain and continue to build your stock of financial security for the long term. In other words, your primary drive is to move up the spectrum, away from poverty into a place of financial comfort and ease.

By the same token, imagine mental health as a continuum between two extremes of, say, suicidal lows and boundless positivity. When you imagine your mental health in this way, you can understand that achieving a state of 'not being mentally ill' equates to our analogy of 'not being poor' on the wealth spectrum. Not being mentally ill does not automatically equate to good mental health. Nor is it easily visible from external appearances.

Performing well in work or school is not a true indicator of good mental health. Many people experience high-functioning anxiety or high-functioning alcoholism, for example. This means they learn how to mask their underlying mental ill health, appearing outwardly to cope or even excel in their work, even fooling themselves that there is no real problem, until they reach a point of breakdown, or realisation that this way of life is unsustainable for them.[5]

The underlying premise of this book is that we can all do things to continually improve our state of mental well-being. Learning about, and gaining expertise in, some of those things is analogous to saving money or investing for the future. It will build your stock of mental wealth resources that will help you during the tough times. When depleted, those resources will need to be restocked.

When practised in this way, it can prevent almost any future life crisis (which we will all experience at some point in our lives) from being the catalyst for falling into serious mental ill health. Instead, it will enable you to draw on inner reserves until the moment of crisis has passed. In my experience, this is possible, and proven to be so in my work with thousands of private clients.

Neuroplasticity

Neuroplasticity demonstrates the capacity we have for continual mental growth and change. By the same token, any change that might be attributed to neuroplasticity can atrophy if not exercised regularly. We see this, for example, in research conducted with London black cab drivers, whose brains become enlarged in the part of the brain responsible for spatial awareness, the hippocampus.[6] Yet, when they retire and no longer need this expanded spatial awareness, that part of their brain reverts to its previous size.[7] Like exercising a muscle to maintain flexibility and strength, we each need to consistently work on mental flexibility and strength, continually building our stock of mental wealth. What better place than education to help us move up this continuum of mental wealth?

Grades and pass rates

The drive to push pass rates and grades as high as you can may seem like a lofty ambition and a suitable measure of success for your school, the students who go there, the teachers who give their all, the policymakers who want to measure everything and for the parents who demand the best. What could possibly be wrong with that?

For some students, there's absolutely nothing wrong with it. For those academically inclined, certain of the future they want, with a supportive family environment, and destined for a traditional profession such as law, scientific research or medicine, it can still be a pretty good ambition.

Most parents love it too. Parents from higher socio-economic groups may have measured their own achievement in terms of exam success, degrees attained and universities attended. They want the same for their children. Parents from lower socio-economic groups may also attribute any economic struggle in their own lives to limited academic success at school. They want their children to achieve what they didn't achieve. Retrospectively, they have bought into the mantra of educationalists and politicians, such that exams and grades achieved remain the holy grail of entitlement and opportunity in life. Since pleasing parents can be one of the hardest parts of the job, this one core of agreement with many can come as a welcome relief. You might, justifiably, feel disinclined to push back.

I have sat in conference halls, listening to impassioned teachers making the very credible and laudable case for maintaining the pressure on students to perform academically, to reach the predicted grades, to attain university places – almost at any cost. As if declining mental health is somehow an acceptable by-product of academic achievement. However, there are signs, annoyingly persistent and increasingly repetitive, that there might be a number of mental health black holes in this bucket of achievement measurement, performance management and strategies for student motivation.

> 'If children feel stressed in tests, it's because adults have told them it's high risk. You should never pass your pressures down to the staff. Staff should never pass their pressures down to the children'.[8]

Doing your best?

There is an unspoken (and sometimes spoken) assumption that young people today are lightweight, not made of the tough stuff previous generations were made of, even labelling a specific generation 'snowflake' because they are perceived as being poor at handling pressure and 'heat'. If you only teach them 'grit' and 'resilience' '(though there's little clarity or genuine understanding of what is actually meant by 'grit' and 'resilience'), they will thank you down the line for making them work hard to achieve those exam passes and grades. However, for too many young people, this approach sets up an abiding sense of underachievement that will plague them into their middle years and beyond.

THE DANGERS OF BOX TICKING

Although we may be encouraged to exercise and eat well, the NHS has limited intensity of focus on prevention. It remains predominantly about treating and managing, and is the last line of defence against government policy that omits prevention from its planning and goal setting.

Why? Because prevention is long term. Politics is short term.

The evidence for this has been catastrophically played out with the lack of appropriate preparation and the inadequacy of early response to the Covid-19 pandemic in the United Kingdom, which left the NHS and care homes exposed with insufficient personal protection equipment.

Having worked in the NHS between 2002 and 2005, I played a part in localised pandemic planning meetings alongside local government colleagues. None of us was expertly briefed or prepared for any kind of pandemic apart from assurance of adequate Tamiflu supplies (avian flu was the expectation).

We were doing what many of you probably do in schools – drawing up a policy so that we could tick a box to say we had one. Next!

Governments may have changed but short termism hasn't.

Whilst there is plenty of researched evidence that mental fitness issues begin with positive family relationships – ergo, parenting – it is not acceptable to use this as a rationale for not taking responsibility for making powerful change within education. If you do, then you are implicitly saying to young people, 'Your problem is with your family. I can't help you'. In which case, you may as well throw in the towel now. Education is *not* the innocent party when it comes to failing mental health in young people and the long-term effects of policies enforced today.

Staff well-being

The tell-tale signs of staff under pressure are absenteeism and teachers leaving. And teachers are leaving the profession in droves – retiring early or moving on to other professions. A research study conducted by the Department of Education (DoE) confirmed what is obvious to the educated lay person. They are primarily leaving because of workload, government policy and lack of support from their leadership teams. There is already the suggestion of an upward trend in work-related stress, depression and anxiety in recent years, according to the Health and Safety at Work Executive (HSE), 20120[9]

In 2018/2019, stress, depression and anxiety accounted for 44% of all work-related ill health cases and 54% of all working days lost due to ill health. In my clinical hypnotherapy practice, I notice the difference first hand. The majority of clients show up seeking help with stress at work, social anxiety, impaired sleep, short temper and poor concentration.

It will be as evident at home and in your staff room as well as your classroom. In short, the drive for improvements to mental well-being should not be restricted to small, identifiable groups or individuals, who experience some kind of symptom of ill health that demands a diagnosis and treatment. It should be extended to every person within the school, including students, teaching staff and support staff.

It starts with you

No head teacher would ever say they don't value staff well-being. However, it gets easily pushed down the list of priorities as attention is focused primarily on budget and curriculum. It's all planned for tomorrow, next week, next term or next academic year. That tomorrow may never come. It's a little like planning to start that new exercise regime after Christmas, after the holiday, after the weekend. You have great intentions, but never follow through with appropriate action.

There's hidden mental health pitfalls at play here too. Decision fatigue is one. Every single time you fail to make a decision about something (anything) on your list, mentally storing it for 'not now' or 'later', the decision-making part of your brain is, nonetheless, taking up valuable thought processing time and space. It fatigues you, increases overwhelm, hinders concentration and focus, and can lead to forgetfulness. In short, you're stress loading by doing nothing instead of something. You're adding a layer of unwarranted stress to your own plate. When that happens, you're more than likely going to pass that to others around you, either consciously (for example, by mindless delegation which increases someone else's overwhelm) or unconsciously (for example, by becoming increasingly unavailable). Your decision-making becomes impaired by the very decisions you're not taking. You can find yourself spending inordinate amounts of time deliberating over relative trivia and postponing high-level decision-making indefinitely.

Knock-on effects

Stress overload can be highly infectious, especially in close working or living environments. School is the perfect breeding ground. If you don't find ways to keep your own stress in check and better manage your mental well-being, eventually the staff room and the entire school culture becomes predicated on symptoms of stress and anxiety.

STRESS AT WORK

The rate of work-related stress, depression and anxiety was broadly flat but has shown signs of increasing in recent years.

- In 2018/2019, stress, depression and anxiety accounted for 44% of all work-related ill health cases and 54% of all working days lost due to ill health.

Doing your best?

- Stress, depression and anxiety is more prevalent in public service industries, such as education, health and social care, and public administration and defence. By occupation, professional occupations that are common across public service industries (such as healthcare workers, teaching professionals and public service professionals) show higher levels of stress as compared to all jobs.
- The main work factors cited by respondents as causing work-related stress, depression and anxiety were workload pressures, including tight deadlines and too much responsibility and a lack of managerial support (2009/2010–2011/2012)[10].

In their own words

What follows is an extract from a longer article in *TES*, written anonymously by a teacher. You may remember it.

Dear Head teacher,

At what point in your life did you make the decision to abandon your soul and become a lifeless, unsympathetic, data-driven robot?

I remember a time when you had character, a sense of humour, a smile!

But now all we mere mortal staff members see is a slick corporate busybody, who seems to prioritise corporate over community, data over duty and money over morals.

Under your merciless regime, your ruthless cronies in senior leadership have adopted a series of strategies for keeping us 'on our toes'.

I suppose it makes sense. After all, we mere teachers are all a collection of lazy, opportunist sluggards who abandon our duty at the first opportunity when we aren't under the constant fear of a visit from a dreaded 'learning walk'.

The pressure of observation

Personally, I love the idea that at any moment of any lesson (usually the most unfortunate and inconvenient of moments) a member of senior leadership will merrily jaunt their way into my lesson to take a snapshot observation (read: judgement), which may or may not be used against me at any point of my career.

The problem with this snapshot is that it is not necessarily representative of me, my teaching or my class.

One of Monty Python's most famous sketches was The Spanish Inquisition. The iconic line was: 'No one expects the Spanish Inquisition! Our chief weapon is surprise, fear and surprise'. Never a truer word. Fear and surprise.

Of course, the Spanish Inquisition was an evil and malicious initiative, which attempted to expose non-believers by catching them off-guard and then bringing them to so-called justice.

I wouldn't dream of making a comparison with you and your senior leadership team. All you're trying to do is expose us as bad teachers by catching us off guard and then

Teacher well-being

I am sure that you would like to believe that, since you've introduced learning walks, I feel a lot happier, I work a lot harder, I sleep better at night and, overall, I am a better teacher.

I take no pleasure in informing you that this is, regretfully, not the case. On the contrary, I am not happier, I do not work any harder, I do not sleep better, and I am not a better teacher. I am anxious, stressed, uncomfortable and unhappy. Which, as I would hope you know, is not the best recipe for a healthy or effective teacher.

Learning walks are just one example of how staff are treated like shit. Whether it is a learning walk or a book scrutiny, it seems that your regime is constantly scouring our work, looking for something to complain about.

To make the situation worse, your top agenda in all areas is data. Learning has been dumped in a river somewhere, while data obnoxiously masquerades in its place.

But what is the cost of this data-driven way of life? Our health, our emotional well-being and, ultimately, our teaching. It costs us our livelihood, and damages our pupils' educations. A stressed, tired and anxious teacher is hardly ever a good one.

Prioritising data over learning

So why do you do it? Why do you make our lives hell, for the sake of data that isn't necessarily even representative of the students' learning?

You used to be a teacher just like the rest of us. Surely you see that what's happening is wrong?

The only answer I can come up with is that even you, in your seemingly absolute position of power, also have a merciless slave-driving overlord who is keeping you up at night, scrutinising your every step, breathing down your neck, haunting your dreams and devouring all of the data you throw its way, while constantly demanding more.

This overlord is a ferocious monster with the annual salary of nine NQTs. It sits in an ivory tower, consuming our resources, while those of us in the classroom are slowly drained of time, energy and will to teach.

In need of a leader

The situation is dire, and morale is low. What we need now in our school is a leader: someone who is able to lift the spirits of the school and remind the staff that what we're doing is worthwhile, despite all the national difficulties and struggles.

We need a leader who is inspirational and sympathetic, motivational and kind, but above all understanding. A leader who gives us slack when we want it, and support when we need it.

We need a leader, not a CEO. As our head teacher, you can be that leader and still fulfil your duty to the trust – I can say that confidently knowing you as a teacher, as a professional and as a person.

Doing your best?

This letter is written anonymously. You might never read it. But you might be reading it now. If you are, I hope you reflect on your position and your duty, and you think about how you make us feel, how you treat us and what you want your legacy as a head to be.

Yours, the unknown teacher from an unknown department.[11]

No school leader would say that the mental fitness of staff was unimportant. On the contrary, you might feel great empathy and even a degree of guilt for the pressure your teachers are under, having to deal with the sharp end of budget cuts and the relentless drive for targets and grades. However, just because you recognise a situation – or sympathise with it – doesn't mean you aren't culpable in helping to create it, or make it worse. Such is the case with staff well-being. If you don't take care of the staff, then you aren't taking care of the students.

Impact on students

Without high levels of positive well-being within the teaching and support staff – in other words, a culture driven by mental fitness at its core – your students are bound to suffer. It is not psychologically possible to protect young people from mental stress and declining mental health if they inhabit a toxic environment where grades, pass rates, pupil numbers and attendance rates come at the expense of everything else. In short, we are teaching young people that they matter less than our precious targets. We might delude ourselves by telling ourselves it's in their best interests, or that pressure is a normal part of life and they need to learn to deal with it before faced with the 'real' world. Yet, it is a lie.

It may be tempting to resign yourself to impotence over government policy and blame that policy for excessive workload. However, you are in the wrong job as a leader if you allow this rationale to colour your thinking and leak into your school culture. You are at the helm. Everyone looks to you for leadership. It's up to you to provide it. Unless you take full ownership and responsibility for the workplace culture in your school, then there is little point in trying to fix mental health problems in young people. Until you assume full, confident responsibility for creating an environment in which teachers feel supported in and out of the classroom, their stress levels will rise and they will be at risk of poor mental health, absenteeism and either leaving your school or leaving the profession entirely.

The problem with continuing professional development (CPD)

Every professional organisation expects its members to continue professional development beyond their qualification. Teachers, you would imagine, would be world-class leaders in setting a standard in lifelong learning. But that's not what I see in many schools. What I see instead is individuals from the leadership team sent to regular conferences and expected to return ready to impart the knowledge they have gleaned from a frantic day diving from one seminar to another. Or expected to formulate a policy based on what they have gleaned in a few short hours, armed with leaflets and presentations, many of which they will never look at again. As if policies and brief exposure to learning equal depth of understanding adequate to embed and share knowledge with others.

Alternatively, staff and visiting speakers or trainers are 'subjected to' twilight 'training'. Having delivered these myself in the past, I have sworn never to do so again. In fact,

44

it's been a driving force behind the content of this book and the imperative to support and enable culture change, working only with the full support of head teachers.

There's so much wrong with this approach, it's hard to know where to start. Firstly, it's like cramming last minute for an exam with accompanying sleep deprivation and virtually no long-term understanding of the subject. Teachers are tired. They've just spent all day battling with teenagers in the classroom and probably have an evening of marking and lesson planning ahead of them. Heaven forbid, they might even, if they're lucky, be planning some personal downtime to spend with family or on sports and hobbies. The last thing they want to do is learn about something they probably had foisted on them that week or that morning. Enforced learning is never great for engagement. It sure as hell isn't good for igniting passion and effecting change. CPD, in my view, should have an element of choice in it. Most professionals choose to deepen their learning with subjects that interest them specifically and intersperse that learning with updating on key techniques or strategies. It's true that those ambitious teachers still driven by the passion that got them into teaching *will* seek out additional learning and put themselves forward for fresh initiatives – but the onus will remain firmly on them doing things in their own time. Which adds to the pressure of work they already experience and limits their capacity for vital downtime – to step away from work and build mental fitness with sport, activity or other leisure interests that stimulate the brain to produce vital neurotransmitters (in particular, serotonin, gamma aminobutyric acid [GABA] and dopamine) to maintain mental fitness.

Then there's *inset* days, which don't seem to get used for staff CPD. Instead, they often get hijacked by the leadership team for varying forms of information dissemination around budgets, targets and policies. Hardly the ideal method for inspiring action and positive culture change.

The villainy of Ofsted and the DoE

Ofsted and the DoE play a double-handed villainous role in the leadership and management of schools. Their 'interference' or lack of it in relation to funding, performance and measurement, is most frequently attributed with the failure of schools to attend suitably to the mental health needs of either staff or students.

I'm not setting out any defence or otherwise of policy planning decisions or the changing demands of government. Having worked in the NHS, I'm all too aware of the negative impact of often ill-informed political meddling, and the flawed decision-making that flows from central sources, who have little to no understanding of what really happens on the ground.

That said, it is way too easy to blame someone else for poor performance, for failures, for anything that doesn't go the way we'd like it to; and when there's consensus amongst peers, we take comfort in the validity of our positions and the impotence we feel in making much more than minor inroads in whole-school or individual performance.

How much sympathy do you have for hearing similar arguments from pupils or parents – constantly seeking scapegoats for the lost or missed homework, for low grades, for the failure to study hard enough, for the poor behaviour or adherence to rules or something else? Forgive me for momentarily lapsing into a stream of clichés. However, playing the blame game disavows personal ownership of any part in being the change that the crisis we are experiencing demands. If you keep doing what you've always done, you'll get what you've always got.

Doing your best?

Effective mental fitness initiatives?

More and more effort gets thrown at the mental health problem. Meanwhile, nothing seems to be enough to stem the apparent growing tide of mental health difficulties amongst students. It is a sad truth that many head teachers, even if they acknowledge privately the impact – good or bad – that mental health has on the wider school performance, on achievements or behaviour beyond the school gates, take little action which reflects this private acknowledgement.

In some cases (not you, reader!), I've heard head teachers refuse to acknowledge that any of this is their problem at all, that it is a health issue for healthcare providers, that the fact they have an onsite counsellor, a quiet room and a (partial) PSHE programme, with occasional assemblies or mental health weeks, is enough. In fact, they refuse to entertain more, because they perceive it is a cost they are unwilling or unable to commit funds to, or they claim their job is merely to educate (aka, get the numbers of desired GCSE passes and grades). Taken to its logical conclusion, this way of thinking implies that mental fitness is not something you can learn or improve. Instead, it is something you magically have or don't have. Which is pretty crazy thinking for someone responsible for imparting learning and a love of learning. This is a fixed mindset[12] rearing its head.

However, it's understandable to want to divest your role as an educationalist from doing any more than is already being done to improve pupil mental health. It can seem that the more resources get thrown at the problem, the bigger the problem gets. And there's some truth in that. Especially, if your school has invested in specially trained counsellors, mentors and therapists to support children showing signs of difficulty, yet the problem seems to escalate, rather than diminish.

Media joins the party and everyone starts theorising about the growth in mental health problems amongst young people, social media being at the forefront of the scapegoat list, with parenting style following closely behind – perpetuating a story that parents believe children can do no wrong, that discipline and rules and structure are non-existent beyond the school gates. Everyone will have a story or two to back this up. The trouble is, when you start to believe that the 'problem' of mental health is outside of your control, that's when it becomes a problem. You can feel like the person holding your finger in the dam; and this necessitates re-enforcements, which come in the form of charity volunteers, counsellors, experts, coaches, mental health leads and more pastoral staff. It may feel like an improvement, but it doesn't really improve things. In many cases, it also involves delegating the problem and that can be a big mistake.

Mental health leads

Since the publication of the government's 2017 Green Paper, 'Transforming children and young people's mental health provision'[13], which outlined new responsibilities for schools and colleges around mental health, there has been a move by many schools to appoint designated mental health leads. It sounds like a step in the right direction. However, sometimes we can allow the decision to appoint a mental health lead become an excuse for abnegating responsibility. It's a little like trying to solve your health and safety problem by simply appointing someone with the title of health and safety lead, sending them on a one-day training course and expecting the whole health and safety of an organisation to change simply because that person has been appointed. That just isn't the case.

Without authority, a title means nothing. Mental health leadership needs exactly that – leadership. It's not just me who says so. The mental health charity, the Anna Freud Centre, has long-standing experience in mental health education in schools. They acknowledge that the mental health lead needs to be a member of the senior leadership team (SLT) in order to stand any chance of embedding or introducing whole-school approaches with any real impact. Without bold leadership and accountability on mental health, which includes a whole-school strategy, you simply perpetuate the problem. That only serves to get you, and everybody else, more and more frustrated at the lack of progress.

> It is not a requirement for the designated mental health lead to be a senior leader, but schools tell us that Mental Health Leads who are either on the senior leadership team (SLT) or have support from the SLT are likeliest to be able to implement whole-school change and improvements efficiently.[14]

Because of the way the brain deals with stress and pressure (which is one of the first things we teach people to understand in our own training for aligning well-being with performance), those frustrations have a habit of growing, which leads to your own stress levels rising. When your stress levels rise, this trickles down through the leadership team into the teaching staff, and back to the very children you are supposed to be helping.

Which brings us back to intervention. The focus of many 'experts' is on getting better at identifying young people at risk so that they can intervene and take action to support those 'at-risk' students. This sounds all well and good (and certainly well intentioned). However, it's here that mental health interventions can contribute to making the problem worse. Resources, effort and thinking get dedicated to managing mental *ill* health, instead of fostering mental fitness. The truth is, the more you focus on something the more it grows.

Measurement and monitoring

The current generation of young people are not only demonstrating greater signs of mental distress and (arguably) lower levels of resilience than their predecessors, but they are also the focus of testing, measurement, observation and assessment than any other generation before them. They've become lab rats in school uniforms.

This, it could be argued, can be one of the many contributing factors to their declining mental health. When you know you're being measured or assessed for something, there is a human tendency for comparison with others, for knowing what's 'normal' and for striving to achieve that. It fits with the model of their social media world – who's normal and who isn't, who performs better than whom, who is cleverer, who is more talented, thinner, cooler, etc.

The truth is, it adds pressure and no amount of teaching on inclusion and diversity will make a difference. After all, if you want to influence effective change quickly, it's not what you say that matters, it's what you do. And there's no point telling young people that difference is to be embraced when you're measuring and assessing their conformity to norms.

Behaviour, exclusion and off-rolling

If ever there were a contentious issue, it would probably be this. Much is written and said about how best to manage 'bad' behaviour and disruption in the classroom. After all, you're tasked with ensuring the school has a published policy, and a harmonious environment is vital to the success of all within the school. Understandably, your own focus might be on considering ways to improve any disruptive behaviour. This could include enforcing even stricter rules and boundaries. However, if there were better understanding of the potential negative mental health impact of those very policies, you might consider a different approach.

Remonstration with unacceptable behaviour immediately starts off on an unsteady mental health footing if behaviours are glibly described as good or bad. That's unhelpful for mental wealth building in two key ways.

Firstly, describing behaviour as good or bad strengthens a fixed mindset thinking in everyone associated with the behaviour. It sets up a young person – or a member of staff – to either win/lose, succeed/fail. This can be demotivating and demoralising for the young person if layered with other stressful, mentally poor circumstances or thought processes (e.g. 'I don't belong' or 'I'm not good enough' or 'I can't do anything right'). They may choose to just give up. 'What's the point?' or words to that effect can then typify any encouragement to change behaviour. The member of staff is equally challenged by all-or-nothing outcomes. Once an ultimatum is set, it becomes almost impossible to explore any other avenue of response. In effect, they are presented with decision-making cul-de-sacs. It's hardly the basis for exploratory learning and mutual understanding, and unless you possess the skills of a mind reader, you have absolutely no idea what the true underlying cause of bad behaviour is. Assumptions are always a poor first base for improving mental health and well-being.

Secondly, unless you tread carefully with your own language and behaviour (and tired staff may struggle to achieve this 100% of the time), it is easy for a young person to interpret your dissatisfaction with their behaviour, as dissatisfaction with who they are. In other words, they adopt 'bad' as a personality trait. They can become, in their own minds, 'bad' people, especially if similar circumstances get played out away from school. When you believe something about your core identity is true, it makes it virtually impossible to change that position with a little motivational pep talk, or a conversation with a counsellor or support worker. Any dressing-down for unwanted behaviour simply confirms their belief that they are 'bad' or worthless. Bad behaviour equals bad person equals continued 'bad' behaviour. Time stretched, overwhelmed and stressed teachers are less likely to spend the time required to fully listen, enquire or explain. It becomes a lose/lose situation. This is powerfully damaging at any time in life, more so in adolescence, which is the time when identity is formed and there's a deep-seated need for belonging.

Here's a brief overview of some of the key mental health pitfalls seen in the way this is managed:

1. Behaviour and discipline

    Often, when we consider behaviour in a school context, it's black or white, good or bad, under control or out of control, acceptable or unacceptable. It's also riddled with inferences and assumptions with which we think everybody else is in agreement. If only that were the case. Of course it's a challenge coming up with effective strategies that support all students equally. However, the underpinning drive for meeting exam and grade targets colours the decisions made around what is or isn't regarded as unacceptable behaviour; how we communicate it and how we respond to that unacceptable behaviour.

Doing your best?

2. Exclusion

It's hard to imagine how routine a process exclusion has become in the life of many schools. It seems to have become almost the first line of defence for a teacher trying to carry out the impossible task of teaching in an undisciplined or unruly classroom. Teaching in a noisy, disruptive environment is stressful. It's difficult for studious children to concentrate and learn. So, the unruly, disruptive child becomes singled out as a problem and excluded. Exclusion can so easily result from rules that are unnecessarily authoritarian or insensitive to the needs of individual young people who may have existing mental health conditions, or have family circumstances outside school which make compliance near impossible – like caring for a family member, having anxiety, living in a low-income household where new school shoes are financially out of reach. Clear boundaries for young people are important, but greater awareness of diversity and inclusion is vital.

3. Off-rolling

Despite strenuous denials, it is true that many schools have used off-rolling to massage their own 'success' figures for exam passes – and to maintain that theirs are schools that do not have problems with poor standards of behaviour or underachievement. They make the child the problem, wash their hands of responsibility for them and export them to bewildered parents, other schools or pupil referral units. In so doing, they put children at risk of being lured into crime through gangs and county lines 'recruiting'. What starts as behaviour that is not managed well in school can cascade into a long-term problem for the child, their family and for the wider community. Off-rolling of vulnerable children becomes a precursor to criminality and long-term exclusion, not just from school, but from society.

Under the pressure of reduced staffing – especially reduced support staffing – it can be challenging to the point of impossible to manage disruptive behaviour in school in order to allow for a good learning environment. However, that bad behaviour can, in part, be predicated by the obsessional drive for exam targets and grades. Too often, children are branded with bad behaviour for minor rule transgressions, which can result in further 'bad behaviour'. Schools sometimes act in ways that are regimental and not necessarily founded in logic or reflective of the world in which young people find themselves.

4. Rules and boundaries

We all know that teenagers, especially, can be full of bravado and act tough when inside they are fragile, scared and vulnerable. We know, too, that they require the security of clearly laid out – and adhered to – boundaries. However, for as long as I can remember, schools use of boundaries is driven more by a desire on behalf of heads to exert control, without being clear on what the benefits are to young people and with no consideration of diversity or inclusion. Many heads and teachers provide little more of a response to the question of 'why?' than 'because I say so' or 'because' or simply batting down any questioning of behavioural rules and boundaries as insubordinate.

I get it. If you want to be able to teach, you need a class to be respectful of the teacher, the class and of one another. You also need to be able to assert authority for those occasions where health and safety demand it. Plus, when you or your staff feel overwhelmed by the time and performance demands placed upon them, they will sacrifice listening

Doing your best?

and empathy in favour of time. However, young people are inquisitive. As their adolescent mind develops, they question the world around them and rightly so. They want to know *why* the rules exist. They need to know that they belong. And they need to believe they have options. Sadly, this isn't how rules or standards of behaviour are presented to them. Too often, relatively minor breaches of rules result in a Mexican stand-off, with neither party willing or able to step down from a point of ultimatum.

Here's an example of a potential teacher–student engagement when both are under pressure:

Teacher: 'Take your coat off'.
Child: 'Why?'
Teacher: 'Just take it off'.
Child ignores request and walks away.
Teacher: 'Don't walk away! Take your coat off'.
Child: 'Fxxx off!' (or similar)
Teacher either chooses to ignore or escalates.

Escalation can involve exclusion from class, isolation or exclusion from school. This might seem appropriate for the behaviour that resulted from the initial request – but it is vital to drill down into the reason for refusal of that first request. Removing coats in school may be a rule – but wearing, or not wearing, one is hardly a serious behaviour transgression. There's so many reasons a child might justifiably question that rule as making no sense and therefore challenge it. They might be cold. They might be hiding dirty clothes (and feel ashamed). Maybe they get bullied for how they look in school uniform and want to hide it. There are so many potential reasons that should be given greater consideration, firstly when creating the rules – and later, when enforcing them. Be honest with yourself and your students. Many rules in school have little learning or logic associated with them, apart from demonstrating an ability to follow rules, any rules. As we'll explore later, this is a tired hangover from a method of schooling that no longer serves the same need in business and society.

> 'Children with mental health problems are more likely to miss school – this can be for a variety of reasons. But the less children attend school, the more out of step with learning and socially isolated they can feel'.[15]

We want young people to listen to us; but do we listen to them? Are we adequately sensitive to signs of hardship, of bullying, of shame? Also, are we adequately factoring in the facts as they relate to the world of work that this generation will be entering upon leaving school? The current generations of young people are growing up in a world where anyone can become successful without rising through any hierarchy, where rule-breaking is almost an essential prerequisite for success as an entrepreneur. Often, rules are predicated on outmoded or faulty thinking about what the world beyond school demands. A perfect example is the stringency on wearing complete school uniform, transgression of which, in some schools, results in exclusion from class. Many different reasons are given for this rule, though few of those reasons are shared with the young people for whom they are intended. The rationale for strict adherence to uniform rules doesn't really stack up. Let's consider a couple of key ones.

50

Uniform thinking

1. The world of work demands formal, smart attire.

In some businesses, this is still true, but it's increasingly rare for business to demand anything beyond smart casual, if that. The world of work most young people are entering is markedly different from the world of work as it was 10, 5 or even 2 years ago. Old school thinking is dying as the technological revolution transforms every working and social norm. Most businesses want employees who are reliable, clean, personable and able to embrace modern technology with ease. The modern organisation is less hung up on formal attire. In fact, in a world where embracing diversity is increasingly demanded, clothing 'rules' could be interpreted as part of an employer's failure to be fully inclusive.

2. Adhering to uniform rules denotes respect for authority and makes it easier to enforce other standards of acceptable behaviour.

This is a particularly thorny one. Is it about the uniform, or is it about the authority? If it's about authority, where are the good reference points and role models we can point to, in order to back up this assertion? Those who are in traditional authority (politicians, bankers, priests and corporate leaders, for example) demonstrate on a daily basis that they can't be trusted with our welfare – or the future of the planet. The news shows us police abusing those in ethnic minorities and reveals priests, health and care workers abusing children and vulnerable adults. Abuse occurs in relationships of authority that are unquestioned and unchallenged. Maybe we need to re-evaluate the rules and boundaries we create with the new world in mind, rather than the old one in which we all unquestioningly trusted professionals and authority figures.

MENTAL HEALTH TRENDS: CHILDREN AND YOUNG PEOPLE

Trends over time can be produced for 5–15 year olds, in whom there has been an upward trend in the prevalence of any disorder (9.7% in 1999, 10.1% in 2004 and 11.2% in 2017).

- One in twelve (8.1%) 5–19 year olds had an emotional disorder such as anxiety or depression.
- This was more common in girls (10.0%) than boys (6.2%), and rates increased with age.
- Rates in 5–15 year olds increased between 2004 (3.9%) and 2017 (5.8%).
  (Source: NHS DIGITAL, 2018)[16]

- Mental health problems affect about 1 in 10 children and young people.
- They include depression, anxiety and conduct disorder, and are often a direct response to what is happening in their lives.
- Alarmingly, however, 70% of children and young people who experience a mental health problem have not had appropriate interventions at a sufficiently early age.
  (Source: www.mentalhealth.org.uk/a-to-z/c/
  children-and-young-people)

Doing your best?

Mental health trends

Many children at risk of suffering from poor mental health pass easily under the radar:

- According to an article in the Washington Post, a report by the Robert Wood Johnson Foundation[17] named the *top environmental conditions harming adolescent wellness* – among them were poverty, trauma, discrimination and '*excessive pressure to excel*', often, but not exclusively, occurring in affluent communities.
- Research, led by the University of Exeter[18], , found that *young people with mental health difficulties were more likely to be excluded (from school)* and also suffer ill-effects from exclusion. The 2017 Mental Health of Children and Young People in England[19] survey reported that one in eight children between 5 and 19 years old had at least one mental disorder. Latest government statistics also suggested that exclusions had hit an all-time high during the 2017–2018 school year with 7900 pupils excluded, equivalent to 42 per day.
- 20% of adolescents may experience a mental health problem in any given year.
- 50% of mental health problems are established by age 14 and 75% by age 24.

If you recognise this long-term impact now and acknowledge the research that supports this suggestion, then you *must* do something about it. Applying sticking plaster solutions to problems that are black holes into which more and more students (and staff) will fall is no better than applying gaffer tape to the gaping hole in your classroom ceiling.

Of course, education cannot be made the political fall guy, responsible for solving all the ills of society, from poverty and distribution of wealth, to crime, weight control, physical fitness and mental health.

Yet, school is the one place where a real difference can be made. It is the one place where there is a chance for fairness to be played out, for kindness to be experienced, for opportunity to be provided, for honesty to be learned, for respect to be given. You and I both know that all of those issues are factors that you, as a school leader, can positively influence more than any other sector or group in society, simply because of the regularity of your contact. Helping a young person overcome the shortcomings of their environment is the best gift you can give. It's what great teachers are known for. It's probably the biggest part of the reason you came into the profession: to level the playing field, to give young people an equal chance in life, to make the world a fairer, happier place.

Early age intervention has been recommended by leading children's mental health charity, Place2Be[20] and it really doesn't require higher-level mental health skills to be able to implement simple tools and strategies that can make a marked improvement. What it does take is a decision, a choice, a shift of attention from spreadsheets to people and a refusal to devolve responsibility for pupil welfare to another person, another group or another time.

When you seize the challenge of mental wealth building in your school as a golden opportunity, rather than a poisoned chalice, it does require you to be bolder and braver. It also offers you the opportunity to rekindle the passion with which you started out. If the Black Lives Matter movement of 2020 has reminded us of anything, perhaps it is that silence and acquiescence are forms of consent. Real change requires real challenge. It requires deeper thinking, wider consideration and radical shifts. Brave leaders know this. I hope you are one of them.

Growth mindset: golden opportunity or fake news?

> A growth mindset is about believing people can develop their abilities. It's that simple. It can have many repercussions but that's what it is at its core.[21]

Possibly one of the main reasons for the growth in popularity of growth mindset, and for seizing onto it as a panacea for positive change in schools and in young people, is the promise of remarkable performance outcomes.

In her TEDx talk,[22] Professor Carol Dweck describes how extraordinarily small language shifts enabled poor-performing schools in underprivileged areas to outperform high-performing schools in privileged areas. Simple. The trouble with simple is that people confuse it with easy. So, when attempts at applying it fail to deliver closing of the performance gap, and when individual achievement doesn't improve, the research underpinning the methodology is blamed and accused of lacking sufficient evidence. Word gets around (teachers talk, I find!) and you see pulled facial expressions of doubt and contempt in casual conversations when the term 'growth mindset' is mentioned.

But this rejection of the evidence doesn't stack up.

The original research was robust and tested extensively at schools within highly disadvantaged areas in the United States. The results, in terms of closing the performance gap, were outstanding. If you watch Carol Dweck's Ted Talk 'the Power of Yet', you'll hear her describe how children in poor areas of New York began outperforming those in highly advantaged schools of Silicon Valley. (She describes them as the 'Microsoft' kids.) In 2007, with fellow researcher, Lisa Blackman, she co-founded a company dedicated to the development of growth mindset thinking within schools and published *Mindset, The New Psychology of Success* (2007, Penguin Random House). By 2010, the US Department of Education was on board, awarding the company $1.05 million to develop the Mindset Works™ school kit.

I have spoken at length with the current chief executive officer (CEO), Eduardo Briceno, who is deeply disappointed at how the methodology has been discredited in the United Kingdom. I am in agreement with him that the problem is not with the quality of the research or faulty outcome analysis. It is with misunderstanding and confused implementation of the research. For example, there is little point in trying to develop a growth mindset in young people when secondary schools operate organisationally from a fixed mindset perspective.

Fixed mindset: the elephant in the room

One of the greatest impediments to successfully implementing a growth mindset is the education system itself. A key characteristic of a fixed mindset is a focus on performance outcomes – pass/fail, succeed/fail, right/wrong, good/bad. The typical secondary school culture is obsessive about measuring performance with constant summative testing, analysing and ranking of students. It's a classic example of expecting young people to do as we say, not as we do. '

> Schools create a certain cognitive dissonance when they proselytise the benefits of a growth mindset in assemblies but then hand out fixed target grades in lessons based on performance'.[23]

Doing your best?

Carol Dweck and Lisa Blackwell discovered that children with fixed mindsets were more likely to believe that they were either good at something – or not – and believe that this could not change; whereas children with growth mindsets were more likely to believe they could improve and learn, gaining expertise with practise and perseverance. This seemingly obvious finding is vital when you consider that beliefs influence how a person behaves, and what kind of life outcomes they will achieve.

It sounds like common sense; and neuroscience adds weight to the argument. During adolescence, the brain engages in what is known as synaptic pruning,[24] deleting the neural connections that are no longer necessary or useful, and strengthening the 'necessary' ones. So beliefs that are reinforced (by environment, school, friends, parents) during the teenage years can be strengthened within the brain. This influences every decision and, therefore, life outcomes. Which is great news if you already believe you can learn, change and improve; and less good news if you think you're future is fixed. Neuroplasticity tells us we can change and grow at any point; but if you don't believe it, it's a bit like having a car and throwing away the key. Put another way, beliefs can be converted to convincing 'facts' within the mind.

Reinforcing fixed mindset

So often, in conversation with teachers, or hearing them speak on broadcasts or social media, you will hear familiar rants about underfunding, overwork, overly stringent measurement and assessment demands – to name a few. Which is not to say I'm in dispute with any of these as 'genuine' obstacles, challenges or constraints.

However, the exasperation that flows from the expression of feeling around them suggests a sense of resignation, a perception of incapacity to respond in any way other than to perform according to the 'rules' of administrators and policymakers. In other words, it demonstrates a fixed mindset.

In turn, those administrators and policymakers operate from a fixed mindset of restricted budgets, need for assessment and performance data. The system is predicated on a fixed mindset. 'This is the way it is'. Depending on which camp you're in (administrator or teacher), you are either: convinced these are immutable, fixed (there's that word) requirements; or, even if you plead the case that they are unnecessary, arbitrary and just plain damaging, you retain a sense that they are fixed and unlikely to change. The real evidence for the latter statement remaining firmly in the fixed mindset camp is that there is little evidence that any positive evaluation of the 'failures' is occurring. Failure and our response to it is fundamental to defining a growth mindset. With a growth mindset, failure is viewed positively. It is seen as an opportunity to learn and adapt, not just once, but over and over again.

Resilience propaganda

Young people, in particular, are often criticised for lacking resilience, for being overly sensitive and, therefore, for being ill-equipped for the world of work and life in general. I do not believe this to be true or fair. Working one to one with young people and adults alike, I find it is not what people lack that is the problem, but what they *believe* they are lacking. There is an enormous difference.

The sense of lack, that you should be something other than you are, e.g. less sensitive to criticism, better able to bounce back from setbacks more robustly, is something imposed from an external source. In other words, the sense of lack ('I am not good enough/smart enough/likable enough') is superimposed by external forces, be they parents, media, teachers or something else. When you tell someone (explicitly or implicitly) that they lack resilience, it is criticism. And since resilience is not a clearly identified behaviour, it is apparently not a criticism of what I am doing, but of what I am being. If you set up a culture or a situation in which a pupil or staff member perceives that they lack resilience, the natural interpretation will be that they are personally deficient in some vital personality characteristic. Let me repeat. They come to believe they *are* deficient.

A sense of deficiency is not a great starting place for building mental wealth or protecting yourself from long-term mental poverty. It sends the message loud and clear that 'You need to be something you are not'. This comes back to identity and your sense of who you are, which quickly becomes your sense of who you should be. Secondary schools, in particular, play a huge part in this, whether to good or bad effect. Initially, a child has no idea what this resilience is (and they may never discover it!), but over time, they are made acutely aware that it is something they lack even if they don't know what it is.

The trouble is that there is no clearly defined agreement for what resilience is or how you build it. Through her extensive and continuing research on growth mindset, Professor Carol Dweck has contributed much to the debate. However, rather than clarify and improve the situation, in many cases, the (wilful?) misinterpretation and misimplementation of growth mindset within schools has served to discredit her work and any powerful learning we might take from it. Many professionals have shot the messenger (growth mindset) instead of allowing it to inform their understanding of school culture, where problems lie and how best to address them.

In brief, Professor Carol Dweck observed a stark difference in mental well-being and success on almost every level amongst people, young and old, based on whether they practised growth mindset or fixed mindset. Those who demonstrate fixed mindset behaviours see life and the world in general terms of good or bad, right or wrong. They respond very poorly to criticism or failure and go to great lengths to avoid either. By contrast, those displaying growth mindset behaviours embrace failure and setback as opportunities to learn and adjust, to do things differently next time. This is one of the core features of successful growth in life, work and relationships (hence growth mindset).

There are two core reasons why, in my view, it has become discredited within the education system in the United Kingdom. Firstly, the education system is, at its core, fixed. The very ethos is one that does not allow for adaptation and change. The only measures of successful school outcomes for either student or teacher are exam grades and passes. Sure, we may talk about the importance of other outcomes, but ultimately, as we've identified in other parts of the book, the only thing anyone is really counting is how many pupils achieve passes at certain grades. Secondly, if the staff attempting to implement the learning associated with a growth mindset are, themselves, powerfully influenced by fixed mindset behaviours, they will not be fully able to engage with the kind of shifts required to liberate students from their own fixed mindset thinking. What – and how – you teach your students now has a far-reaching impact beyond Year 11 or Year 13 and has nothing to do with grades or numbers of exam passes.

Not convinced? Here's an example of the kind of long-term fallout that occurs as a result of a fixed mindset:

Doing your best?

> *As someone who has come to specialise in working with menopause anxiety, I see many outwardly successful women, experiencing debilitating self-doubt and fear of failure contributing to extreme anxiety and loss of confidence in midlife. Their perceptions on life are polarised to all or nothing, success or failure, never or always. It leaves them feeling trapped and frightened and many give up highly rewarding and well-paid roles because of it. This is typical of fixed mindset behaviour, and the thinking which prompted it didn't spring from nowhere. It was learned early on in life and colours their entire lives. They have learned to become high-performing women. Yet, they experience a midlife crash when hormone deficiencies deplete the body of the supplies of serotonin and dopamine which have been propping up this 'faulty' belief system for so long. It leaves them feeling inadequate and helpless, instead of capable and coping (all or nothing).*

I realise some of you may argue that I am skewing the argument and that the whole purpose of education and learning is one of growth, ergo a growth mindset is a common feature and a given. However, when was the last time you encouraged a student, a member of staff or yourself to risk failure or to celebrate getting something 'wrong'? The whole language around learning is around right and wrong answers and, even as far as graduate level, a student is not rewarded for independent thinking. They are rewarded for correctly remembering and referencing exactly who said or did what and constructing a good combination of sentences, exercises or experiments around a topic.

Sadly, too many schools have rejected the whole concept of growth mindset for those reasons. Instead of embracing the positive change it offers for the long-term future and benefit of young people, we default back to the status quo and fall into fixed mindset behaviours, based on the assumption that you can't change things, instead of risking any temporary drop off in 'success' metrics in pursuit of the long game of success and fulfilment.

Identity vs. behaviour

There is another core problem here, as it relates to resilience – and that is the way growth and fixed mindsets are also spoken of and applied in terms of 'being' rather than doing. It is common for people to describe themselves or others as being either fixed or growth mindset. The moment you talk of being something, you are attaching to it a sense of identity. Identity-level thinking is harder to influence and change than behaviour-level thinking. If I am taught that what I am doing is reflective of fixed mindset thinking, but that I can practise using a growth mindset to do something differently, I am aware it is now a skill that can be learned, not an immovable attribute that I have (like a bent nose or brown eyes).

If you are careless about the language you use to talk about growth mindset, turning it into an all-or-nothing attribute that you cannot change, you set up immediate resistance within yourself and within others.

Also, children are very smart (irrespective of their exam grades or passes!). They see straight through incongruity and hypocrisy. So, if we tell them they need to adopt growth mindset behaviours, yet we evaluate their success and judge them according to how many passes they get or what grades they achieve, they will never buy into the snake oil you are 'selling'. Your message and your behaviour (ergo your culture) must be congruent to stand any chance of success.

Doing your best?

Impact on staff

There is another huge elephant in the room when it comes to understanding resilience and improving the mental wealth of our schools. It is that many people interpret resilience as the ability to better endure hardship, to soak up pressure, to 'toughen up', take the knocks, respond positively to criticism, to 'cope' and keep going when the going gets tough. This resilience means you can ride out any storm.

However, what this broad-brushed definition does is allow inappropriate workplace and teaching practices (and metrics) to endure without challenge. It can be used as a smokescreen which perpetuates poor practice, including expectations around long working hours, non-existent work–life balance, imposition of unreasonable deadlines, fear of speaking up, difficult working conditions and bullying. No teacher or head teacher has the right to demand greater resilience when working or studying in a toxic environment.

It is the role of a leader to work to create conditions conducive to supportive relationships, work–life balance and flexible accommodation of diverse needs – for staff and pupils. No excuses.

Resilience can be learned as a preventative tool to enable individuals to remain stable – or to bounce back more quickly – from the likes of unpredicted, unplanned major life shocks, such as illness, divorce, death, change of home. It is not a tool or skill which ensures you effortlessly endure repeated criticism, remain upbeat in the face of chronic difficulty understanding a topic or look on the bright side and think positively about the fact that your father is an alcoholic and your mother just lost her job.

Any way you can support empowerment goes a long way to helping a young person (or any person) become self-sustaining mentally. It equips them with the core skill for building their own mental wealth long after they leave your school. It's a life skill that keeps on giving!

The key to success in mental wealth building is always to simplify a situation and focus on one core question, whatever the situation, circumstance or person: how could tomorrow feel better than today?

This cultural weakness in the system leads to ineffective results and outcomes, which, unsurprisingly, do not match Professor Dweck's original research. This seems to result in the research being publicly rubbished – and steps towards positive culture change being jettisoned in favour of old faithfuls, such as PSHE guest speakers, well-being weeks, special assemblies and positive thinking posters. In other words, doing what we've always done.

Current mental health tactics: the pick-and-mix approach

Below is a fictitious thought process that might typify many an overstretched head teacher's approach to the thorny issue of improving mental health in school. You may recognise many you know within the lines of the text.

> *PSHE? Excellent. You'll use that to cover us for safeguarding, internet safety, bullying, exam stress, self-harm and anything else that becomes topical. We'll do our best to invite local charity and free expert speakers to cover each topic in our single weekly classes across the year, although occasionally, we may have to push the boat out a little and invest in a higher profile national speaker or organisation.*

Doing your best?

To keep costs down, we'll invite them to speak at an assembly, speech day or to take part in our annual Mental Health Week.

If we're up against it on grade or exam targets, we'll drop PSHE for Year 11. They need the extra time for core curriculum subjects. They need to get used to handling pressure too... they'll be expected to perform in the big wide world beyond the school gates, so it's important they acquire a little grit and resilience now. Let's involve head of sports in safeguarding or as mental health lead. After all, they are well placed to develop grit and resilience (and have more space in their timetable).

We have a school nurse, a quiet space and a school counsellor or coach, or at least a member of staff who can double up as one, saving on budget. Honestly, it's all very well expecting us to improve our mental health, but we've no money for extra staff, books or even photocopying, so don't try selling me some Utopian hogwash about how we could do more.

We run regular after school and lunchtime well-being classes, like yoga or fitness, for staff too – and, when budget allows, the deputy heads and heads attend conferences on mental health, so they can come back and share their learning through staff meetings and twilight training.

Honestly, there's not much more we can do... and it's not our job to plug the gap in funding for mental health and, in particular CAMHS (Children and Adolescent Mental Health Services) in the NHS. I'm here to run a school and deliver education. That needs teachers, not mental health experts.

We're doing everything we can to get young people the qualifications that will ensure their future financial well-being, as well as doing our damnedest to manage social inequality and close the performance gap with limited resources.

The real problems you want to address are funding, social media, parental responsibility and Ofsted inspections.

For many head teachers and academy boards, the use of varied short-term tactics, rather than longer-term cultural change strategies, is the norm. Strategies that are wide ranging, ambitious, inclusive and part of a bigger plan of implementation are less common. You will have worked in schools – or currently lead one – where what exists is a set of ramshackle tactical mental health endeavours designed to tick boxes, to justify to inspectors, policymakers, governors and parents, or prospective parents, that work is being done, that the mental health of children in the school is of paramount importance, and that there is a cohesive, well-thought-through, robust plan for their well-being and their positive life outcomes.

Deep down, you know that isn't really true, is it?

Despite the best of intentions – and I don't doubt you have great intentions, otherwise you would not have picked education as a career choice – what you probably have is a pick-and-mix bag of tools thrown together over time – or in a hurry – that give people a sense of security in the short term. The intention is to convey that mental fitness is (a) important, (b) managed appropriately and (c) part of the wider education of students.

Few schools have a genuine, cohesive and responsive strategy dedicated to (a) putting mental fitness at the heart of everything the school does; (b) helping staff and students manage and move up their own personal mental wealth continuum; (c) increasing knowledge and skills for personal well-being for all – that is carried on into future life and enhances positive future outcomes (again, for both staff and students); (d) continual adaptation and improvement; and (e) expanding the potential of the school and everyone

Doing your best?

in it. If you can, hand on heart, say that's what you are aiming for, here's a high five. Huge congratulations, I applaud you. Well done!

Below is a classic example of what can happen when a school puts performance ahead of well-informed mental wealth building strategies. It's based on a real school, though I won't of course be naming names.

The mental health lead and deputy principal was doing a pretty acceptable job of managing the overall health and well-being of staff and students. She involved her colleagues in decision-making and initiatives and practised good old-fashioned empathy and personal connection with students to the best of her ability.

Was everything mental health in the school perfect? Of course not. We're talking real people here. However, she and her team were doing a lot well. They felt empowered to make decisions and manage budgets wisely. They brought in experts to support them when necessary and weren't afraid to genuinely involve parents (in a positive way) or to get things wrong, own up to it and learn from it when they did (growth mindset, anyone?).

Then, along came a new head. An ex-professional sports player who convincingly persuaded the trustees that he had boat loads of expertise in motivation, resilience and a healthy dose of growth mindset and goal achievement factored in, probably based on his experience on the receiving end of sports psychology. I'm sure it all looked good on paper and great in the interview.

But then after a few months in post, there were a few 'unexpected' staff departures in the well-being team. Some might argue this is normal 'new broom' settling in. However, staff inset days were soon replaced by twilight training and fresh initiatives started to slow down as people began fighting internal fires and feeling the need to justify every decision, instead of remaining open to innovation. Creative thinking began to be replaced by defensive policymaking. Effective safeguarding was being superseded by an emphasis on arse covering. The school has become a powder keg of unexploded mental health drama for staff and students alike. Yet, it will take some years before anyone realises and wonders what went wrong.

A word on sporting staff and mental health

The role of designated mental health lead often falls to a teacher in the sports department. I couldn't say why with any certainty, but I'll hazard a guess. The mental health benefits of physical activity are well documented and well researched. The problem is that a teacher who loves sport and understands all of the many benefits that accrue from practising it, may not be too sympathetic, or empathetic, with the many students who don't like it, irrespective of what those reasons might be. Rather than increasing mental well-being by getting children active, what can happen instead is increased alienation of any adolescent who doesn't fit the required sporting personality. This can diminish their stock of mental wealth and damage the self-esteem of children who interpret their lack of skill or interest in sport as a character deficiency, and evidence of lacking self-worth. There's also a commonly held belief that a correlation exists between someone's ability to excel in team sport and their ability to be a valuable, contributing team member in completely unconnected environments. This is a popular piece of hearsay, but also an absurd fallacy that can further damage a person's sense of isolation and alienation for the long term.

Doing your best?

Remember that building mental wealth – or increasing mental poverty – is a layering exercise. Something that seems small or insignificant to one person could, literally, be the straw that breaks the camel's back for another. Empathy is the single most defining attribute in supporting mental wealth building or identifying signs of mental poverty and distress.

I'm not here to knock sport or sporting ambition. Far from it. However, it's vital to understand the distinction between what elite sports people require and what ordinary people require for physical and mental fitness – and not confuse the two or apply broad-brush thinking and tactics to all children expecting identical outcomes.

Seven common mental health intervention strategies and their value

Here's a breakdown of seven of the most commonly deployed mental health tools and tactics in use in secondary schools today.

1. Counselling

   Pros: Counselling has institutional legitimacy within the health sector and it can provide considerable short-term value to young people who may have no other outlet to share their feelings. For this reason, there is nothing intrinsically wrong in including it as part of an in-school mental fitness and pastoral package.

   Cons: There is little research evidence that counselling provides any great improvement in mental fitness over the long term (see below). It is also a time-consuming and therefore costly tool set. Working on a one-to-one basis, with growing numbers of young people seeking help – and, rightly, being encouraged to seek help – can result in an overload of demand, with a school counsellor carrying the burden of underfunding and supply within the health sector. This is, perhaps, why many school leaders, rightly, object to 'picking up the slack' of NHS underfunding. This overload will also take its toll on the professional concerned and they too can suffer their own mental health difficulties in the form of burnout.

   > In 2003, a review of clinical trials showed that counselling provides short-term, modest improvements in reducing anxiety and depression, compared with 'usual care' (routine visits to a GP, CBT and antidepressant drugs), *but no long-term improvements*. A more recent review, by the highly respected Cochrane organisation, investigated whether counselling was effective for mental health and 'psychosocial' problems or 'problems in living'. The analysis of nine trials showed that counselling was more effective than routine visits to the GP in the short term (one to six months). In the long term (seven to 36 months), though, it was no longer as effective. Counselling also failed to have an impact on patients' short or long-term social functioning, such as work, leisure activities and family relationships.
   >
   > *(Source: www.independent.co.uk/life-style/health-and*
   > *-families/counselling-doesnt-work-long-term-taxpayers*
   > *-money-cognitive-behavioural-therapy-a8045566.html)*

2. PSHE

   This is a well-intentioned initiative that is, sadly, treated as an optional bolt on to what many heads perceive as the more serious job of education – as if, somehow, PSHE is not education. Little value seems to be placed on it, except amongst the appeared or self-elected staff who deliver it. It seems that the minute you take an exam qualification away from a subject, it loses relevance. At worst, it's treated as a disposable, slightly irritating add-on that eats into the academic timetable.

Pros: At best, it's a single lesson per week on a plethora of important topics that can vitally influence the well-being of a young person – including safeguarding online, self-harm, grooming, drug use and knife crime, to name a few. It's better than nothing, one might argue.

Cons: It's a drop in the ocean when it comes to really influencing, safeguarding and transforming behaviour. It's a little like providing a one-off English lesson and expecting it to impart long-lasting learning.

3. Assemblies

Assemblies can add value and are the key opportunity to reach the whole school – or large sections of the school at any one time. Given that head teacher teaching time is pretty much a thing of the past, they can also be rare opportunities for the head teacher to establish any kind of a relationship with the students in their a care.

Pros: Assemblies can be a useful vehicle for delivering key messages on wider topics such as mental fitness. There will invariably be at least one student who benefits and seeks support or changes behaviour as a result of hearing something inspiring that touches them.

Cons: However inspiring or charismatic the leader of an assembly is, if information is delivered as top-down communication, its potential positive impact is diluted. It also relies on a school culture of openness and empathy in order to have a positive impact.

4. Guest speakers

Pros: A well-chosen outsider can be powerful in effecting change. It's nice to have, a useful add-on on specific topics, such as suicide prevention, speaking up about mental health, bullying, self-harm, depression, drug use, internet risk, etc.

Cons: It is hit and miss, random and not possible to plan for anticipated outcomes. In some schools or year groups, it can sometimes be the only mental well-being education a student will get. In my experience, it rarely forms a constituent part of a wider, planned strategy for improving knowledge around mental fitness.

5. Mental health first aiders

Pros: Any programme providing improvements for school staff in building their mental fitness know-how is to be welcomed. Feedback from participants appears to be mostly positive and they seem to appreciate new-found confidence in identifying and responding appropriately to a young person struggling with mental fitness issues.

Cons: This remains an intervention strategy, rather than a prevention strategy. There is also a danger that many schools will see investment in this one initiative as a whole solution, rather than a piece of the jigsaw.

6. Charities

Pros: Some wonderful charity initiatives and resources are available in the mental health space for young people and for schools. Working collaboratively with you and your SLT, and aligned to your own wider mental health strategy, they can provide invaluable levels of support and training at a reasonable cost.

Cons: Without clearly laid out service-level agreements and head teacher involvement, the potential of their offering can be piecemeal and scattered, threatening to diminish any positive impact they might otherwise help you to achieve. Working with more than one charity can also be counterproductive and confusing if they

Doing your best?

adhere to different mental health and well-being practices and principles (of which there are many).

7. Mental health leads

Schools have been formally and informally appointing mental health leads for some years, although they may have been called pastoral leads. Although some act as full-time professionals, budget constraints mean that these pastoral leads are invariably expected to carry out this role in addition to their 'main' job. These staff may have been encouraged and supported to gain greater knowledge and expertise through attendance at conferences, webinars and seminars. Mostly, they would probably develop additional skills and input (like most dedicated teachers) through their own personal effort, interest and connections. Meanwhile, continued media coverage of the 'mental health crisis' in schools has prompted government ministers and education/mental health professionals to produce a mental health leadership master's degree for teachers aspiring to professionalise their interest and for schools to have some kind of exam-verified performance measure. The first course of its kind was launched in 2018, with the first cohort of graduates in 2019. This is both good news: professionalising the role in schools – and bad news: many heads may see this as a good reason to devolve all responsibility for well-being to a single person.

Pros: It offers a career path with recognised professional expertise. If the appointment is made at a sufficiently senior level, the person can provide much-needed support, guidance and effective implementation strategies for the head teacher.

Cons: In too many cases, the role has fallen to people outside the SLT and/or to members of the sporting faculty. Presumably, the logic is that, either they have more timetable availability to take on additional responsibility or, as physical fitness professionals, the assumption is made that they will also have a knowledge of, or alacrity with, the fields of positive psychology and mental well-being. Rarely is this the case. With little or no additional training or education in anything other than sports psychology (if that), the problems of young people can be under-reported. Too many students end up labelled as lazy, moody, uncooperative, lacking in team spirit or similar, with little effort to seek deeper answers to behaviour not conforming to the demands of a specific sport or game.

Diversity, inclusivity and exclusions

Diversity and inclusion are the latest 'trends' in acceptable social behaviour. It is no longer a 'relatively' simple case of providing so-called equal opportunity. Organisations are expected to conform to new standards of diversity and inclusivity. This means that our school and business communities should both reflect the broader make-up of society within their membership and encourage inclusion of each individual within the normal functioning of those organisations.

You might argue that your school is already doing so. Sadly, it is more likely that your school merely perpetuates exclusion and division by failing to support young people adequately with confident development of their own identity.

Equality of opportunity is a blunt instrument for change because it simply reflects the status quo, rather than play an active part in changing that status quo. This is evidenced by the appallingly slow rate of change in the representation of women and ethnic minorities on the boards of businesses, in the continuing pay gap more than half a century after it was made unlawful to pay a woman less for work of equal value and in the woeful under-representation of people from lower socio-economic groups within higher education and, therefore, within elite professions, which are disproportionately represented by Oxbridge graduates. These include the BBC, as well as finance and business consultancy.

If you want to make a positive difference to potential outcomes for pupils, you have to get good at understanding diversity and inclusion – and making changes to your systems and processes that improve both.

The rationale for extending the requirement beyond diversity into inclusivity or inclusion is because diversity does not necessarily engender inclusivity. If this were the case, there might be little excuse for social unrest, inequality of opportunity or social isolation.

A school is more likely than any business to meet diversity requirements because it, theoretically, serves the community within which it resides. That diversity will, of course, vary from district to district, village to village and town to town. However, if there is a locally balanced spread of gender, race, sexuality, ethnicity, social class, etc., then the secondary school is most likely to reflect it.

However, just because diversity exists, this does not infer inclusion.

Not so long ago, I was asked to write an online programme for a young business consultancy specialising in increasing diversity and inclusion. It was called 'Embedding Inclusion in Every Day'. The rationale for their business mission and direction was that practising diversity and inclusion didn't just tick a box for data collection. Nor did it solely signify positive employment practise, demonstrating a commitment to be an equal opportunity employer, even though they believed passionately that equality and diversity mattered. No, the real reason they were in business – and what they wanted me to help convey in the course I was being asked to write – was that research had shown that businesses which were truly inclusive and embraced diversity created a commercial advantage. Those businesses which formed part of the research operated in tightly regulated and highly competitive, homogeneous financial markets. Yet, the handful of organisations which reflected diversity and inclusivity on their boards and management teams actually outperformed the competition. It appeared to impact directly on their bottom line. In short, it makes sound commercial sense to practise inclusion.

Now, why do I tell this story? What earthly relevance does it have to your school and the staff and pupils in it? You might think your school culture is inclusive and might feel affronted at any suggestion that this might not be the case.

But, here's the main point. No school culture or management team can be successfully practising inclusivity in an environment where conformity is demanded and, ergo, exclusion becomes the norm. No school – or business – can truly create an environment where individuals achieve their fullest potential unless the people who run that school or business reflect potential and possibility for 'people like us'. Our understanding of personal potential, identity and entitlement is learned best, not through instruction, but through immersive observation.

I learned a lot researching the material for the programme I created – and from the business which had tasked me with creating it. It made me realise how ill-equipped education is – and always has been – for sparking a belief in opportunity, for learning about self-value, for building self-esteem, for building the firmest of foundations for achievement.

On the contrary, most schools, despite best intentions, are hotbeds of intolerance for any person who sits below an accepted norm of achievement or behaviour. This might seem an absurd criticism. After all, we live in a society governed by rules, laws and regulations and a requirement for some degree of conformity to those in order for society to

Doing your best?

remain democratic, pluralistic and safe. Schools, it can be argued, provide a sound basis for the expectations of society at large.

The difficulty is that society itself is changing more quickly than the rules that govern it. Young people have access to the very tools of that rapidly changing society – and there is a mismatch between what they see and experience in the world outside – and what they see and experience inside.

It might not be so problematic if it hadn't been for the increase in school leaving age to 18. Schools now have to work with young people who are adults, who, justifiably, choose their own identity, beliefs and values – and yet are required, on occasion, to suspend that expression of their identity, those beliefs and those values, in order to conform to a set of expectations and standards that may not best serve them in their endeavours to pursue the career, lifestyle or education of their choosing.

In effect, the rule is that you can choose that, but not here. Not in my school yard. What perpetuates is the values of a middle class, aspiring, at best, to be a professional class. Education is not to create the entrepreneurs or employees of tomorrow but to persist in serving the needs of old-style employers today.

Anarchy? Yes, probably. But sometimes anarchy is required. The move from rural, agricultural living to mass urban industrial society that typified the changes wrought by the Industrial Revolution was not easy, comfortable or quick. It transformed the lives of all and in many cases transformation during that change was painful. It was not called a revolution for nothing. Perhaps no wars were fought, but, nonetheless, a revolution occurred. People's lives were turned upside down and upheaval is not welcomed by many.

Old-school educationalists and their policymakers risk being the Luddites of the current technological revolution. These thinking, rules and systems are designed for a world that is rapidly dying out; however, unlike the Industrial Revolution, which had around 150 years to create change, this revolution is happening in tens of years. Rather than fight it or stand like a deer in the headlights, it is our role to embrace it, grow with it, respond to it, adapt. We will make mistakes, get much wrong, but adapt we must.

It is no longer your job to maintain the status quo, but to be a part of the change that is occurring, to support and prepare young people to do what other generations did not and could not, to stimulate the imagination and belief beyond traditional boundaries and limits. Thinking is where the major change needs to occur. Changes and upheaval on the planet, in technology and society are a challenge to our old ways of thinking. Pandora's box is open and there is no closing it now.

Permission to demonstrate and test original thinking has, until now, been held as the preserve of university research departments. The intellectual hierarchy refuses to acknowledge original thought from outside its own confines – until such thought is so widespread and endemic that it cannot ignore it. Our existing culture does not afford the time for chronological, time served, foundation-based learning. In fact, it could be argued that this was ever the case in the Industrial Revolution. Those who effected change did not wait patiently to be given their chance, to ensure they had studied long enough in appropriate disciplines or wait for official approval and permission from the ruling elite. Instead, they took their chances, learned according to their passions and commercial leaning. They thrived on old-fashioned scientific learning, from trial and error, from mistakes, sometimes from recklessness, always from a growth mindset.

Education must embrace and cultivate a culture of celebrating failures and mistakes and teach young people how best to learn from those failures and mistakes. However, if teachers and educators confine their own thinking and systems to acceptable norms of education and learning, designed to cultivate a workforce of paid factory workers and administrators, they will not enable the kind of original thinkers who could make a difference. The truth is that we need our young people to be free from constrictions to creativity and thought, so that they, unlike us, will be able to forge a path of change that saves their own future, as well as our own and that of the planet.

Notes

1 Source: https://sethgodinwrites.medium.com/stop-stealing-dreams-4116c7dbff7b.
2 https://digital.nhs.uk/data-and-information/publications/statistical/mental-health-of-children-and-young-people-in-england/2020-wave-1-follow-up.
3 www.tes.com/news/what-if-schools-valued-well-being-more-results.
4 Source: Brene Brown, *Dare to Lead*, 2018, Vermilion.
5 For further explanation, see www.verywellmind.com/what-is-high-functioning-anxiety-4140198.
6 Source: www.ncbi.nlm.nih.gov/pmc/articles/PMC18253/.
7 Source: https://discovery.ucl.ac.uk/id/eprint/1310481/1/1310481.pdf.
8 Source: Estelle Morris, Halcyon Education podcast, https://halcyon.education/podcasts.
9 https://www.hse.gov.uk/statistics/causdis/stress.pdf. This has been updated to a 2020 report.
10 (Source: Work-related stress, anxiety or depression statistics in Great Britain, 2019, Annual Statistics, Health and Safety Executive (HSE), 30 October 2019, www.hse.gov.uk/statistics/causdis/stress.pdf)
11 The author is a supply teacher in East Anglia. Article reprint permission granted, www.tes.com/news/what-i-wish-i-could-tell-my-headteacher-0.
12 See p. 84: 'Growth mindset: golden opportunity or fake news?'.
13 https://www.gov.uk/government/consultations/transforming-children-and-young-peoples-mental-health-provision-a-green-paper.
14 Source: www.annafreud.org/schools-and-colleges/5-steps-to-mental-health-and-well-being/leading-change/prepare-for-change/.
15 www.mentallyhealthyschools.org.uk/risks-and-protective-factors/school-based-risk-factors/absenteeism/.
16 https://digital.nhs.uk/data-and-information/publications/statistical/mental-health-of-children-and-young-people-in-england/2017/2017#summary.
17 https://www.washingtonpost.com/lifestyle/2019/09/26/students-high-achieving-schools-are-now-named-an-at-risk-group/.
18 https://www.exeter.ac.uk/news/research/title_774208_en.html#:~:text=The%20research%2C%20led%20by%20the,suffer%20ill%2Deffects%20from%20exclusion.
19 https://digital.nhs.uk/data-and-information/publications/statistical/mental-health-of-children-and-young-people-in-england/2017/2017.
20 https://www.place2be.org.uk/about-us/news-and-blogs/2019/may/the-case-for-early-intervention/.
21 Source: Carol S. Dweck, *Mindset*, 2012, Robinson.
22 Source: Carol Dweck, *The Power of Yet*, September 2014, Tedx Norrkoping, Sweden.
23 Source: Carl Hendrick, https://aeon.co/essays/schools-love-the-idea-of-a-growth-mindset-but-does-it-work. Carl Hendrick, 11 March 2019.
24 Source: Sarah-Jayne Blakemore, *Inventing Ourselves, The Secret Life of the Teenage Brain*, 2019, Penguin.

Chapter 4

Winning strategies

Finally, you've reached the point in the book where you get to explore what you can do to change things for the better. Now you can explore the wide range of winning strategies at your disposal.

Whilst you might assume that so much of the book has been taken up with elaborating and honing in on a myriad of tactics, policies and behaviours that don't work, that this is a book couched in negativity, the very antithesis of what it sets out to achieve, we are about to dive deep into the ways in which you can make a big difference. Sometimes, making that difference requires the tiniest of shifts which add nothing to your workload but generate exponentially productive results. The plan now is to foster a greater sense of positivity, hope and courage in you as a leader, such that you can cascade this through your school, in ways that pervade every nook and cranny, every corner of thinking in the minds of your support staff, your teaching staff and, of course, your students.

The last thing you want and need is another 'expert' telling you that you could do better. It's easy to criticise and not so easy to be in the firing line, living on your wits and lurching from one moment of crisis and reactive planning to another, especially when much of that crisis and reactive planning seems to have little to do with the actual education of children, which was why you entered the profession in the first place. The excessive challenges of managing the ever-changing landscape of Covid-19 and unpredictable or last minute government shifts have made this even more difficult.

Before the start of each new school year I suspect you are in school, organising and planning, meeting with your senior leadership team (SLT) and support team, readying the school for an influx of new and returning students.

I recommend you make one key change, one that your primitive mind will probably kick and scream at in resistance, but which will dramatically improve things for you if you trust the process.

Spend one week alone in the school before the return of any staff. Engage in quiet contemplation, meditation. Consider your own expansive long-term goal setting. This involves what business coaches sometimes describe as setting big hairy audacious goals (BHAGs). Think in the long term. Focus on a single huge goal rather than on multiple goals, such that the smaller goals are steps along the journey to the bigger goal. What this key goal becomes is a core decision-making tool.

DOI: 10.4324/9780429353420-4

Winning strategies

Here's how this works. Distractions or alternative 'opportunities' will inevitably appear along the way, so you need to reference how they fit with your key goal. If they take you off in a different direction, you will need to say no. No matter how good an opportunity looks, if it isn't aligned with the achievement of the core goal, it is a distraction and a divergence. Let it go.

Here's an example of what a personal BHAG might look like: to become the key person of influence in mental fitness for education, which includes being awarded a Member of the Order of the British Empire (MBE) (or higher) with published papers and leading an entire training or education programme for other education leaders throughout the United Kingdom and further afield. Or an example school BHAG could be: to become the standout model school for mental wealth building in the United Kingdom, that journalists want to write about and parents flock to send their children to, that students love to attend and that alumni remain committed to. Of course, some of those 'opportunities' may come attached to powerful external influences. This means you need to become good at articulating your goals and the route to achieving them, such that others can buy in and share your vision. Without shared vision, organisational goals will never be fulfilled and personal goals may get jettisoned as unworkable on the way.

Start with you

It may sound trite but the step before the first step in your whole-school strategy is to focus on your own mental wealth. Remember that there is no black and white, on/off switch between mental ill health and mental health. We are all somewhere on a continuum and you are more empowered to identify what initiatives or changes might help others, when you are more self-aware of your own state of mental health and the resources at your own disposal. Whilst there is no one-size-fits-all toolset for individual well-being, the further along the mental wealth continuum you are, the better you can see where change is required and what changes might work; plus have the alacrity to alter a path and try something new if the first path of choice doesn't quite go to plan.

The reason this is so important – and missing this step will set you up for failure – is because when we are low on the continuum, we make poor decisions, we doubt our own judgement (it's clouded by overwhelm and excess of adrenaline/cortisol production) and we seek to blame or find solutions outside of us, rather than access our own resources. How is this relevant to you, as a head teacher or senior leader?

Well, I have yet to meet a person in the education system who doesn't tell me about the pressures that teachers and head teachers are under. They will explain to me about the demands of Ofsted, local authorities, academy boards, parents and, finally, students. In so doing, they are buying in to a logically appealing story that provides a get out of jail card for failure to make dramatic improvements in mental well-being amongst staff and students. The argument is that I couldn't possibly understand, as an outsider, that no one outside the education system has either the knowledge or the right to provide guidance. In the words of my own father, arguably I 'have no conception'.

However, I believe I do, and I have two very good reasons for saying so. Firstly, I've experienced work within the public sector, both in local government and within the National Health Service (NHS). I have supported chief executives in managing communications and complaints, running the gamut of conflicting demands from members of parliament (MPs), local councillors, senior clinicians, the press, members of the public and patients. I am fully aware of the way individuals in each of these groups can attempt

68

to make life very hard, and how difficult it can be to get on with the day-to-day task of delivering the level and quality of service the organisation is intended to deliver. This was particularly so working within the NHS at a time when their public persona was not quite as pristine as it has become under the stress of Covid. Not so long ago, the NHS was an easy target for opposition politicians, the press and the public which made clinicians defensive. I see a similar drama played out in schools, with a similar set of stakeholders often making unreasonable demands that land squarely on the shoulders of head teachers and cascade down through the SLT to every member of the teaching and support staff. My intention is not to negate or deny that pressure or those conflicting and unreasonable demands, but rather to demonstrate that when you focus on one core objective (the well-being of students), decision-making and fronting up to vociferous stakeholders becomes a simpler choice. Leadership is riddled with difficult choices, but if you have a core mission and purpose, this becomes the barometer for every decision you make.

Once you decide where you stand and others know where you stand, it becomes a clearer path of communication. Does it prevent objection, disagreement and attempted obstruction? No. Does it give you good reason for standing your ground and greater confidence in doing so? Yes.

In the NHS, there is only one measure of success – patient welfare. There may be disagreements about what that welfare looks like, but, as someone with a strong background in customer service, the patient, not the clinician, is the best arbiter of what their welfare looks like. In the case of a person under 16, that decision maker becomes the parent. Sure, they may need help to make an informed choice, but ultimately it is their choice.

In the same way, you may well be an expert in education, but it is still the student (and, because of their age, the parent) who is best placed to make a decision about their welfare, not the local MP, not Ofsted, not the local authority, not the SLT. All of those groups are ultimately answerable to an electorate, which comes back to the parents. People become confused by legislation which makes it the case that the law and by proxy, the decision makers who uphold that law (you, the head teacher and the local authority) are the best arbiters of a child's welfare. Safeguarding helps prevent a child's welfare falling into grey areas, where inappropriate parenting (or teaching) means the parents' rights can be over-ruled, but the rule of thumb should be that the child, ergo the parent is the best arbiter of well-being.

Impaired decision-making

Stop overthinking it.

You're in a culture that is driven by measurement reporting policies, structure and organisation. There is an important requirement for systems and structures and consistency. However, the very part of you that has probably got you this far in the school system can actually be a handicap in making the kind of simple, yet powerful changes required to make a success in building a mentally healthy culture that you can be proud of because it supports staff and students alike.

Again, stop overthinking it. I realise that you probably want me to give you a step-by-step strategy that includes creating new policies and measurement systems and additional training of staff to supplement their existing skills to make the biggest change. When what you really need is to do something very simple and that's change the way you think. It starts with you. If you can resist the temptation to call a meeting, to request or write a report, to put together a detailed plan, and instead just take on board the lessons in this book about how you personally improve your own state of mind, strengthen your own internal toolset, then you will be in a far better place to influence and kick-start

Winning strategies

the very change that's required to benefit. An inspiring leader doesn't overthink how to inspire. They simply dive in and get on with it. That's your key requirement here.

Lots of leaders love the idea of a 'to-do' list, a checklist of actions you can take that will lead you to your destination of a mentally healthy school. That, you might argue, is what will prevent you overthinking it. Just tell me what actions to take and I'll take them; but it's the 'action' piece that is missing the point. Whilst there are mentally healthy actions we can take – exercise, being in nature, meditation – what's important, as a leader, is that you first embrace the Zen philosophy of the 'empty cup'.

Before you continue to reiterate that it's different for head teachers or education, let me explain an aspect of the way the brain works to demonstrate how your own thought processes contribute to amplify the problem – or see easy solutions.

The role of your reticular activating system (RAS) and mine!

Our RAS means we see what we want to see. Let me explain, using an example you may well have come across in some distant training on an inset day or even in general conversation.

Imagine you have ordered a brand new red car. Almost the moment you order it, you suddenly see them everywhere. They pop up in every car park, on every street and every motorway. It is as if a graffiti artist has been busy with a spray can, turning the world of cars red. You had no idea they were so common.

Nothing, of course, has changed, except that the part of your brain, called the reticular activating system, has now been primed by your conscious decision to focus on that particular piece of information.

The RAS is responsible for filtering sensory information through every part of your body. Of course, at any one time, you are bombarded with sensory information from the outside (and inside) world. In every moment, your mind and body are scanning and aware of every sensory input. For example, the light coming in to your right eye, the blood flow in your left foot, the saliva in your mouth. Your conscious mind (the part responsible for making all those key decisions, like which shoes to wear today or what time to set the alarm) can only manage around three pieces of information at any one time (and queue the rest). The effective functioning of the RAS means your conscious mind can remain blissfully unaware of any of the subtler sensory inputs without having bottlenecks which would prevent normal day-to-day functioning and higher-level decision-making. It simply filters them out of your awareness.

You only become aware of the light coming into your right eye when someone suddenly comes towards you with full beam headlamps on as you drive, aware of the blood flow in your foot when you've sat too long in a single position and experience numbness or tingling, or aware of the saliva in your mouth when the dentist has your mouth filled with implements.

The way in which your RAS filters and prioritises information to your conscious mind is based on novelty and curiosity first. However, safety and responding to threat trump all other inputs. Any safety information gets through unfiltered; a person stepping off the pavement ahead of you, for example. Its second priority is to filter information you tell it is important to you, through your thoughts, habits and actions and a continual process of what I describe as 'pattern matching'. Think of something once and it's likely to be filed away without much reference. However, once you start actively engaging

Winning strategies

with a situation or a thought, you tell yourself a story about it that can trigger chemical reactions in your body, which can trigger emotions. Those emotions and those chemical reactions elevate the importance of the thought or situation and the associated emotion and chemical reaction. The cycle continues until we become distracted or choose to move on. However, the more we revisit similar situations, thoughts or circumstances (as perceived by the RSA), the more embedded the emotional and chemical response becomes, influencing the pattern of our thinking (and our certainty around it). The evidence for its existence lives within our own mind but we perceive it as evidence of 'truth'. Why? Neural pathways are created. If we don't travel those pathways (think that similar thought, have that similar experience) often then they remain temporary – like walking once in a cornfield. The beginnings of a path open up as we walk through it, but quickly grow back if it's a one-time or infrequent event. However, travel that path often and the brain starts making synaptic connections, strengthening well-trodden pathways and increasing their significance (and truth!). If strong emotions are part of the story that connects the pathway, it changes your neurology (through neuroplasticity) and becomes an autopilot response for you.

So, if you spend a lot of time engaged in heated conversations at home, with colleagues, on Twitter, in boardrooms or elsewhere, you are hardwiring a 'reality' based on a world view which may not be valid. If those conversations increase your stress levels, the pathways become even more hardwired, entering the 'safety' realm managed by the RAS to prioritise emotional responses, and bypassing usual critical thinking.

What this means for you (and your staff and students) is that once the amygdala sounds the alarm, cognitive function, such as learning, problem-solving and creative thinking, cease. This has been described as the amygdala hijack (Curriculum Management Solutions Inc., 2018[1]) and the better known, fight, flight or freeze response.

Do not make the mistake of assuming any higher level of logical reasoning trumps this primitive response mechanism. It doesn't.

In other words, the more stressful your own mind-body responses and emotions, the more likely you are to make poor decisions, have clouded judgement and be unable to see clear solutions. It's like being stuck in a cul-de-sac with a sabre-toothed tiger, engaged in constant combat or avoidance strategies with no way out. The longer you remain there, the more hopeless and helpless you become. Your amygdala (the powerful guard dog of the brain) reacts in a split second to the first sniff of any kind of social, emotional or physical threat. Once 'threat' is perceived, it is activated and bypasses all other systems in the brain to send distress signals in the form of the stress hormone, cortisol.

BRAIN FUNCTION SUMMARY (AND ITS ROLE IN MENTAL WEALTH/POVERTY)

- The brain is unlimited in its capacity to learn and rewire itself. All brains. For everyone.
- Novelty, which might pose a threat or a reward (physical, emotional, or social), is detected by the Reticular Activating System (RAS) and communicated to the amygdala. Threats throw the amygdala into action and derail all other cognitive processes as the body defaults to Fight, Flight, Freeze or Appease. …. the challenge is to help students (*as well as self and staff*) to feel safe enough to avoid an amygdala hijack so that learning

Winning strategies

> *(plus personal growth and mental wealth building)* can occur. *This goes for you too. YOU ARE NOT IMMUNE!*
> - Cognitive challenge, novel problem-solving, and physical activity stimulate myelination which makes complex tasks both easier and faster.
> - Practice strengthens and deepens learning; a lack of practices results in the brain pruning unused neural pathways.
> (Source: https://curriculumsolutions.net/blog/2018/02/28/culturally-responsive-teaching-how-the-brain-can-hijack-learning/. Author's notes in italics.)

On the positive side, the neocortex region of the brain, though comparatively slow in processing information, houses our executive function. It is the command centre that manages working memory and controls planning, abstract thought, organisation and self-regulation (though the act of self-regulation is weaker amongst adolescents, whose brains differ from those of adults). Nonetheless, it has an effectively endless ability to learn and rewire itself and it is here that we build our intellective capacity – our brain power. If, that is, we can get past the RAS and the amygdala! This applies to everything from resources, to solutions and problems (and yes, of course that includes me, but since I am seeing solutions and possible workarounds rather than problems and accommodation of those problems, I would argue it's a more helpful form of confirmation bias).

There are things we believe that we can change because we have control over them. There are things we believe we *can't* change because we *don't* have control over them. However, sometimes our RAS distorts the difference between the two. We can convince ourselves of things we cannot change (that, with a shift of perspective, we can). This is fixed mindset thinking and an organisation instilled with fixed mindset leadership will find it more difficult to foster widespread growth mindset in its staff and students. Young people may not yet have the full wisdom or knowledge that comes with age, but no matter what age you are, it is relatively easy to sense incongruity or hypocrisy, both of which can be damaging to a young person's well-being. The very best form of learning (and one that feels 'safe' to the primitive mind) is one that comes from following role models. Leadership by example is the most powerful form of influence. Your words have restricted power unless they are accompanied by congruent actions. If we see our leaders fearlessly taking on the wild bears (metaphorically speaking), we will feel more empowered and confident in our own abilities to do the same, and our safety in doing so. Anything which contributes to calming the primitive mind, so that it doesn't fire off the fight, flight or freeze response, is conducive to maintaining healthy mental fitness and warding off anxiety. No matter what you might convince yourself of privately regarding your skills at wearing a mask of calm or serene confidence and control, students will sense that something is not quite right. They will smell something is off. It will unnerve them at a subconscious level and contribute to overloading their own stress buckets. It will add fuel to the fires of anxiety. Never underestimate the impact of leadership decisions taken in the confines of your office. Staff and students alike *always* know when something is awry.

Examples? You might think you can't change the way you implement a curriculum based on your interpretation of the Department of Education (DoE) guidance. This is especially true when there's collective or shared agreement on this as a fact amongst colleagues and fellow head teachers. However, if we can take any learning from US and global politics in the past year or decade, it's that truth and facts aren't exactly the same for all parties. I'm not suggesting that you or colleagues are remotely deluded in your judgement or that you ignore guidance issued. On the contrary, I'm suggesting that it's possible that there's another version of truth you could create, a version that works better for you and your staff and your students.

It's really important to understand how this approach and this way of challenging the status quo is a vital cog in the machinery of improving the positive outcomes of your students. This includes their mental fitness and their career chances. Your willingness at all times to remain curious, rather than frustrated, when things don't quite go the way you expected and hold the perennial open question in mind of 'what *is* another way?' is pivotal in embedding a growth mindset in your school. Become it. Model it. Watch it proliferate.

Unwittingly, as you move up the career scale or into adulthood, it can be easy to slowly switch off the curious, open mind that education requires and that inspired you to study and become a teacher. Because it happens slowly, you may not notice it occurring. Worse still, you might convince yourself that that curiosity and open mind is no longer of any value in the regimented world of educational leadership. You cannot then expect pupils to easily engage their own curiosity and wonderment if you have quashed your own. It smacks of hopelessness and helplessness, neither of which are mentally wealthy feelings.

This is why every page of this book is imbued with the implied request for you to change your own thinking and build your own mental wealth reserves in order to create the very school and students it will be a pleasure to lead and an exemplar for others.

Let's look at some of the changes you can make, starting today, that don't require a raft of consultants or specialists to be roaming your corridors, writing reports, observing lessons and making onerous recommendations.

Proven strategies

A recent systematic review which looked at 17 individual project evaluations specifically asked: do school-based, universal mental health promotion interventions improve children's mental health and is it possible to identify attributes that are common to successful interventions? The review found that it is possible to have a positive impact on children's mental health through school-based programmes. The most positive evidence of effectiveness was for programmes that adopted a whole school approach, were implemented continuously for more than a year and were aimed at the promotion of mental health rather than the prevention of mental illness. Those programmes which measured self-concept, emotional awareness and positive interpersonal behaviours rather than conduct problems and anti-social behaviour were more likely to show moderately positive or positive results. Methods of delivery varied and included behaviour change techniques; involvement in co-operative/helping activities; training of teachers; training of parents; changes in school environment, systems or culture. It is worth noting that all but two of the studies in the review were carried out in the USA, and that the authors point out that while the results support the feasibility of the school mental health component of UK national policy, they do not of themselves show that these programmes work in a UK school setting.[2]

Winning strategies

Culture change: quick fixes

Managing positive behaviour in school is for the good of individual children and for the benefit of the school community. (Notice the use of the phrase positive behaviour, rather than good behaviour. It's an important distinction that I'll draw on throughout the book. Language is powerful and it's important to choose our words carefully at all times. We know this when it comes to behaviour around exclusion and inclusion. It's equally important in consideration of good mental health, confidence and resilience. Used ineffectively, it's a subtle form of unconscious bias and exclusion. Used effectively, it forms part of a framework of subtle, but integrated culture change for an entire school community.)

Rules – options. One of the many skills young people will need to develop as they enter the adult world is the art of good negotiation and compromise. We need to be able to negotiate in all kinds of relationships at work and at home. Rules at school and expectations around behaviour are ideal learning platforms, if we choose to see them that way. Sadly, it's more likely that breaches of rules result in a Mexican stand-off, with neither party willing or able to step down from a point of ultimatum.

The physiology of stress

When someone experiences a stressful event, the amygdala, an area of the brain that contributes to emotional processing, sends a distress signal to the hypothalamus. This area of the brain functions like a command center, communicating with the rest of the body through the nervous system so that the person has the energy to fight or flee.

After the amygdala sends a distress signal, the hypothalamus activates the sympathetic nervous system by sending signals through the autonomic nerves to the adrenal glands. These glands respond by pumping the hormone epinephrine (also known as adrenaline) into the bloodstream. As epinephrine circulates through the body, it brings on a number of physiological changes. The heart beats faster than normal, pushing blood to the muscles, heart, and other vital organs. Pulse rate and blood pressure go up. The person undergoing these changes also starts to breathe more rapidly. Small airways in the lungs open wide. This way, the lungs can take in as much oxygen as possible with each breath. Extra oxygen is sent to the brain, increasing alertness. Sight, hearing, and other senses become sharper. Meanwhile, epinephrine triggers the release of blood sugar (glucose) and fats from temporary storage sites in the body. These nutrients flood into the bloodstream, supplying energy to all parts of the body.

All of these changes happen so quickly that people aren't aware of them. In fact, the wiring is so efficient that the amygdala and hypothalamus start this cascade even before the brain's visual centers have had a chance to fully process what is happening. That's why people are able to jump out of the path of an oncoming car even before they think about what they are doing.

As the initial surge of epinephrine subsides, the hypothalamus activates the second component of the stress response system — known as the HPA axis. This network consists of the hypothalamus, the pituitary gland, and the adrenal glands.

The HPA axis relies on a series of hormonal signals to keep the sympathetic nervous system – the 'gas pedal' – pressed down. If the brain continues to perceive something as dangerous, the hypothalamus releases corticotropin-releasing hormone (CRH), which travels to the pituitary gland, triggering the release of adrenocorticotropic hormone (ACTH). This hormone travels to the adrenal glands, prompting them to release cortisol. The body thus stays revved up and on high alert.[3]

We can't control what goes on in the external world, however much some people try to convince themselves that they can. The truth is that death, war and disease happen; relationship breakdowns happen; crime and abuse happen; flood, fire and drought happen. Any of these events would cause a spike in the physiological stress response. In other words, we experience an increase in adrenaline, which causes a rise in blood pressure, sweat production and pulse, and a decrease in digestion.

With consistent everyday stressors, such as exam pressure, friendship difficulties, hormonal changes and problems at home, the mind and body are creating a chronic environment in which it becomes hard to focus, to think clearly. Emotional responses, such as anger, frustration and upset, are triggered faster.

Many people are unable to find a way to put the brakes on stress. Chronic low-level stress keeps the hypothalamic pituitary adrenal (HPA) axis activated, much like a motor that is idling too high for too long. After a while, this has an effect on the body that contributes to the health problems associated with chronic stress.

Once people around you start reacting to the behaviours generated by that chronic physiological stress, it only compounds the problem, because it layers stress upon stress.

Whole-school thinking

Develop a plan for what you really want to achieve in life and in your school. Now screw it up and think bigger. Develop a plan for what you want the staff and students of your school to achieve in the longer term, for the real potential you'd like them to fulfil, so that your original plan is just a minor stopping off point, a potential stepping point, the first ripple in the pond if you like. Hell, make it even bigger than that, if you feel driven to. Whatever you do, stop thinking small and talking yourself out of things before you've started.

This is unleashing the bigger thinker, the person who knows how to dream big, but has maybe lacked the courage to do so in the past. Perhaps you've talked yourself into a mindset that says you're powerless within the system. It's easy to do and you won't be alone. There's comfort in numbers, after all.

Maybe you recognise yourself or others as having retreated behind the secure doors of long-standing routines and tried and tested systems. Perhaps you're proud of 'metaphorically speaking' getting good at colouring within the lines. But you also know that something is wrong. Very wrong. The system is broken. And you also know the familiar definition of insanity. It doesn't work but you keep doing the same thing. The only way to change things is to stop doing the same thing and start doing something different. Very different.

This is your moment. To be a trailblazer, an advocate for fresh thinking, a new way. There won't be just one way. There will be many ways, some better than others. Are you ready for the challenge? Someone has to be. Why not you? Big change requires brave action. Bold steps taken by the few can lead to major shifts. Think Rosa Parkes or Ghandi. Seriously.

Winning strategies

You don't have to have any idea of how the hell you're going to carry out this big ambition, but you have to set it as a marker, a true vision. You have to share it with those around you, your staff and governors, your Ofsted inspectors, your academy board, your local politicians, if you feel really bold. Sell it to them all. Encourage staff and students to embellish and expand it, make it even bigger. Open it up for contributions from all. Just like a brainstorming session, no idea is a bad idea, no early criticism or 'buts' are permitted. All is encouraged, acknowledged and captured. At this point, nobody needs to know how. They just need to consider what.

Now you step back. Capture the key ideas, the vision, nail your colours to the mast. Use this vision as your whole-school objective. Make it prominent in the school. Use every communication tool at your disposal to build advocacy, so that those big and crazy dreams start to feel like possible goals and objectives. And make them exciting.

Encourage ownership of the big ideas amongst staff and students. You're the leader, but not the pack horse responsible for carrying everything. None of this works without everyone on board. Gather your connectors, identify other leaders. Give them responsibility. Give them space to be heard. Give them space to fail and learn; and share that learning.

As you step out and raise your head above the parapet, like-minded people will emerge. Not immediately. To begin with, you will be, like me, a lunatic raging against the machine. But hold firm, hang on tight. You can do this. Others will join you. They just need a little time. Learning will also come from failure – I'm afraid you also step into the vanguard of this particularly powerful mode of learning. Embrace it. Throw your first pebble in the pond. It doesn't matter which one, just any one.

In their own words

Anonymous Year 11: what could help?

Bring it down to our level. We don't understand how the real world works because we're protected by parents and teachers. Teach us in a fun way – songs or concert – about mental health. That helps me the most. We need a person we can be comfortable talking with, someone we can trust, open up to, have a bond with, someone who knows exactly what we mean because they've been in that situation.[4]

Looking for a framework?

Building mental wealth for an individual or a community is not achieved in a single step with a single tool. Rather, it is achieved, as I will continue to repeat, by first changing the way *you* think and fostering powerful ways to amplify your own growing confidence, in ways that empower others to do the same. Once you see the startling changes and benefits that are possible when you make simple changes within your own thinking and behaving, you will have greater insight and commitment to finding ways to introduce those same strategies within your school.

I was reluctant to include any kind of rigid structured framework within the confines of this book. Why? Because within that framework, or rather the desire for that framework, I recognise a desire amongst head teachers and policymakers for safety. There is a fine line between systems that empower and free – and systems that constrain and confine. As a leader, it is your job to distinguish between the two and to continually review (which doesn't mean another excuse for delegation or further introduction of admin-heavy, life-draining processes). Like learning to kayak or sail, my job is to show you how. Your job is to navigate the river. No framework in the world will alert you to every current, whirlpool or eddy in its ever-changing flow.

Beware. The primitive mind is wily. It will encourage you to resist anything it perceives as risk-taking (which, in this case, is nothing more than a new perspective). Changing nothing can feel safer. However, this is the very part of the mind which is most dominant in creating the bedrock of anxiety and mental ill health. What this means for you is that, under stress, you will bypass the very part of your mind responsible for good decision-making. Which is bad for you and bad for the school.

So, with great caution, and with an empty cup, I offer you the Anna Freud Centre Five Steps Framework[5] as the basis of your own framework, though I will lay out my personal perspective and recommended adjustments in the pages that follow. If you aren't already familiar with the framework, you might want to take some time to visit their site, which lays out the basis of their work in a simple to digest format. It's a free, well-researched and evidence-based resource that prevents you reinventing wheels.

If you're a lover of checklists, you'll like the format. It's basically an online spreadsheet using a traffic light system to track progress. It ticks the box that every academic seeks – an evidence-based framework. In other words, no one can criticise you for adopting maverick thinking that isn't supported by other academics. There's safety in that.

Remember, of course, that the best strategy is always to create mechanisms that help others find their own path. Prescriptive guidance, in my experience, is always less powerful. This is partly because the same tools and techniques do not work in the same way for all people. It is also because, as human beings, we are better able to follow through with something that is our idea, rather than doing what someone recommends you do – especially when that person is a parent/teacher/boss!

You can adapt your approach with the additional simple tools shared within this book to create a simple system that empowers each member of your school. It can become a flexible skin that grows and adapts according to the needs of the school and every member of it, rather than a rigid straitjacket of a framework that, once in place, can never be altered without resorting to lengthy retraining, policy updates and vacuous reporting measures.

Rather than replicate each step, I will add commentary or elucidate on each of the key points as they relate to the contents of this book. Unsurprisingly, the first step is about leadership – the entire ethos of this book. In this, I am in complete agreement with the Anna Freud Centre. Where we differ, perhaps, is in adapting proposals around leadership and process in order to meet the demanding requirements of a modern secondary school head. I understand this and I empathise. It is not an easy role, but then did you ever think it would be? Let's visit each of the steps in the Anna Freud Centre Five Steps Framework to consider how you might adapt them to make them even more powerful. If you dive deep into every part of the Anna Freud Centre resources provided, you will gain some of the best access to information and knowledge you can find. However, it is likely that leaders pressed for time will skim read and access some of the information or resources, rather than all. It is on this basis that I have reviewed the steps.

> At the Anna Freud Centre we aim to equip schools to respond to the individual needs of their community and create a culture that supports emotional well-being and resilience. Our 5 Steps approach will support schools in embedding a curriculum that enables pupils to become well-rounded individuals through opportunities for personal and academic growth.[6]

Winning strategies

Step 1: leading change

One of the key proposals is to appoint a designated mental health lead, which is also a recommendation from the government's Green Paper, 'Transforming Children & Young People's Mental Health Provision'.[7] Whilst you can make any person in your school a designated mental health lead, including governors, the trickiest aspect is to avoid the temptation to add it to an existing role or job description without making any provision for changes in workload.

If you choose to make an appointment within your existing staff structure and employ gentle arm twisting or play on someone's natural enthusiasm, generous spirit or passion to take on such a role, without reviewing how this sits within their other responsibilities, you are falling at the first hurdle. Remember that every action and decision you take within your school from now on needs to be taken with the consideration of mental well-being and its positive impact on performance at the forefront of thinking. That means that every decision will impact on you, your teaching staff, your support staff, parents and students. It's no more daunting a prospect than the myriad of decisions and priorities you've been balancing to date. Yet, it will possibly prove more rewarding and you will be grateful for the first decision you took to make this the focus of every moment. Forgive me for a moment if I adapt the saying that 'a dog is not just for Christmas, it's for life'. A decision to focus on conscious mental wealth building (rather than mental health management) is a continual process, and it is not just for students. It's a decision for you, your team, for every day and for life.

Step 2: working together

I cannot stress enough the importance of this step. In particular, the Anna Freud Centre recommends including pupils, staff, parents and carers in decision-making. I highly recommend you consider utilising the resources they have available. They have done much of the work for you.

Mental wealth building is life itself and, as such, is both a solitary journey and a collective one. You have to focus first on you as an individual, endeavouring to build your own skill sets, habits and attributes in mental fitness. Your own environment is the only one you have conscious control over in terms of what you do, how you do it and the outcomes you achieve. Sometimes, outcomes may deviate from what we intend, but on the whole, we achieve something close to what we set out to achieve if we are clear about our intention at the outset and stay true throughout.

You can make all the rules you like, you can monitor, record, reprimand, challenge, but ultimately, the behaviour and responses of others are outside your realm of control and jurisdiction, no matter what it says on your business card or your payslip. Nonetheless, you do not live in a vacuum. You will impact people you come into contact with fleetingly and people you come into contact every day. Most of the time, you will have no idea at all of the nature or long-lasting effect of that impact. Many is the time I have bumped into people or received messages months and years down the line to discover that something I said or did impacted them hugely. Thankfully, in a good way. However, there will be many who do not get in touch, who, I have no doubt, will have been equally impacted in a negative way. You will have the same stories and experiences. The thing is that we can only do what we feel is right and hope for the best.

The power of involving others in the process of positive change and embracing new ways of thinking and behaving that are supportive of good mental well-being is that

Winning strategies

when we are involved in decisions and choices, we are more committed to the outcomes and will work harder towards them. You do have to be willing to listen, to be vulnerable, to open yourself up to change you might not have opted for if it were entirely down to you, but the aggregated outcome will be infinitely better.

Some heads may have a tendency to think that strong leadership means making decisions, which devolve into delegated tasks cascaded through a top-down hierarchy. Time pressure can make this more likely, even amongst well-intentioned heads, whose natural style of leadership might more naturally be collaborative. However, this kind of leadership, borne out of expediency can quickly shut down all future, valuable contributions from others. It only takes three occasions of modelling a certain behaviour before that behaviour becomes an accepted cultural habit or boundary within a relationship. For example, say you host a meeting and, in the dying moments, ask for contributions from others, only waiting a hair's breadth of a second for a response before rushing off to your next appointment. In so doing, you shut down contribution. The pattern has been set. You cannot hide behind a veil of justification based on 'I asked and nobody contributed'.

- Great leadership is, in my view, the same as great mental health leadership. Great leaders put trust in the people around them. This invokes greater trust in you and in themselves. Building trust in oneself is a key feature of mental wealth building.
- Great leaders listen closely to people around them. This allows people to feel heard and to contribute. People who feel heard are less likely to feel inadequacy, rage and resentment, each of which contribute to diminished mental wealth and store up long-term problems, which may or may not be diagnosed as mental ill health issues, but will limit someone's ability to live a happy and fulfilled life, where they live up to potential, without a nagging doubt that maybe they have nothing worth contributing or saying (because no one ever listened before).
- Great leaders reflect and consider, without procrastination and prevarication. They model decisiveness. Indecisiveness diminishes mental wealth so any part you can play in modelling the alternative works in favour of building the mental wealth of those around you. The caveat is to avoid it becoming a smokescreen for disempowerment in others. Good decision-making also needs to be devolved in order to build a stock of mental wealth in others.
- Great leaders take tough decisions when they have to. This demonstrates courage and makes people around them feel safe. Great leaders are unafraid to reveal vulnerability which tells the people around them, we're in this together. They foster a sense of belonging. Belonging is one of the base requirements in Maslow's hierarchy of needs. Without it, we cannot move higher up the scale to personal fulfilment or achievement. It is equally a core factor in building your stock of mental wealth.
- Great leaders nurture the people around them to ensure great leadership prevails when they can no longer lead. This instils a sense of empowerment in others, who strive to fulfil their own potential.
- Great leaders share their vulnerability in ways that, rather than making them weaker, make them stronger. They model and encourage others to be open, confident in the knowledge that it is safe to share your vulnerability and this does not handicap your progression through life. If there's anything most teenagers fear, its vulnerability. If there's one time in your life when you might choose to wear a metaphorical mask of 'I'm okay, nothing wrong here', it is adolescence. Sadly, for some, that mask remains into adulthood and throughout our entire lives, limiting the capacity to fully savour each moment and feel able to 'risk' failure (the very learning which sets us up for

Winning strategies

true success) or anything which might fall short of perfection. These are key factors in some of the more embedded mental poverty behaviours. They can lead to underachievement and playing small, or high achievement with accompanying imposter syndrome (which can lead to burnout or breakdown). I am sure you have many student examples who fit each of those categories. Demonstrating vulnerability as a leader also requires you demand no less of your leadership team. However high performing someone is outwardly, if they are unwilling to share their own vulnerability, they are an accident waiting to happen and a potential liability. They can become bullies at work, or demonstrate intransigent behaviour, teaching and work practices – which benefit no one and can demoralise or damage the fragile, developing mental wealth of the adolescents in their field of influence. Never allow someone's academic gifts to come before their emotionally healthy and mental wealth building behaviour.

The Anna Freud Centre, quite rightly, recommends the involvement of, not just staff, but also parents, guardians, support staff and governors. Please don't use the shortcut of establishing a policy that you then 'share' or 'communicate' with parents, pupils and governors when what you're really doing is simply showing or telling them about decisions and actions that you have chosen to take. This may seem obvious, but having worked alongside and within public involvement teams within the NHS, I know that this is a very common strategy. Just setting up a big meeting, inviting people along, publicising it and allowing questions to be asked does not constitute involvement. It is rubber stamping, it is outmoded, potentially inflammatory and insulting. I have seen this in local and national government organisations too, so you wouldn't be alone – and might not even get criticised for embracing just such a practice. However, you would not be demonstrating good mental health leadership that puts the mental health of staff and students at the heart of your organisation. You cannot be responsible for the welfare of every person, but you can do your best to employ the best tools, techniques and strategies to the best of your ability. Work put in at the front end (soft, thinking time) pays off big time at the back end. If you spend more time on the overall mission of improving well-being, and dedicate yourself to no more than three core objectives each day, week, month and year, you will be more successful and satisfied in the long run and so will everyone else.[8]

Step 3: understanding need

What's most important to understand about this step is that it need not be the priority. Too many schools want to jump straight in here – and it's why so many think that it isn't really their problem, but a health problem. They become frustrated and spend too much time and money on ill-thought through solutions to plug the hole in the dyke. These include employing counsellors and inviting in paid professionals to deliver one-off or ad hoc training to staff or pupils. It doesn't work and, if anything, it compounds existing problems, or even creates new ones. For example, inviting someone like myself to deliver a two-hour talk on the root cause of anxiety to a tired group of teachers at the end of a school day, simply fans the flames of frustration and irritation, exacerbating the very anxiety you wish to find ways to alleviate. Used in isolation, these tactics are sticking plaster solutions to gaping wounds. It's a little like the football manager of a struggling club investing in a star player in order to resolve morale problems in the dressing room. There's nothing intrinsically wrong with buying star players. It's part of a manager's job to do so. However, it's about using the right strategies in the right place at the right time.

80

Winning strategies

As with most things in life, timing is everything. By all means, recruit a counsellor or invite professionals in, but evaluate what the bigger picture is before deciding who that best person is, and when the best time is to solicit help. Avoid the knee-jerk, 'it's a mental health issue, so I need a mental health professional' response, or the response that regards the problem as 'sick' children who need support. This is starting at the sticky end of the stick. Starting from a place of building mental wealth instead of fixing mental ill health changes everything. Start with you and build on out.

Also, there's a risk in attempting to 'identify' children at risk of mental ill health that it becomes another measurement and data capture exercise that yields little more than others and stokes the fires of pathology. The more you look for problems, the more you find them (remember the RAS), and the more you risk encouraging them. Trust me when I tell you that your biggest problem is chronic stress. Deal with ways to manage that effectively and a big chunk of your problem will be solved. I have personally worked with thousands of people, young and old, who have conditions ranging from mild anxiety or insomnia to severe obsessive compulsive disorder (OCD) and eating disorders. My first line of attack is always to help eliminate chronic stress. Whether they started out with chronic stress or developed it along the way, the truth is that, because it creates a situation where the primitive mind takes over, clarity of thought is diminished. They cannot take good decisions, cannot concentrate, memory is affected, to name a few key indicators. No one is in a position to consistently perform effectively on any level when they are under chronic stress, but they start to see the way forward when you help reduce that key component.

And there is no hiding behind the argument that stress is a normal part of life and that we need to become accustomed to it, and handling pressure is a key part of exam performance and achievement at school and in life. There is an ocean of difference between the positive impact of occasional stress and pressure, and the kind of chronic stress which students and staff are expected to live under in the modern school (and I'm aware that includes you!).

Step 4: promoting well-being

This is one of those steps which many schools may choose to take in isolation, but this would, in my opinion, result in a series of compromise solutions and piecemeal 'fixes' or changes. You might justify this on the basis that to take up *some* initiatives is better than to take up *none*. It's hard to argue intellectually with the assumption that something is better than nothing. However, when it comes to mental wealth building, I'm not really sure it is. For me, mental wealth building is an all-or-nothing strategy. You can't partly improve a mental wealth culture. You either commit to improve it or you don't. I say this only because I've witnessed some of the (in my view) worst types of implementation where highly dedicated and very capable members of staff are parachuted in to the mental health cultural equivalent of a war zone and expected to improve the situation with a few personal, social and health education (PSHE) lessons, a bit of counselling, a mental health week and a couple of assemblies.

Let me choose an extreme example to illustrate why I think this way. This is a little like an abusive partner in a relationship arguing that giving the abused partner a regular sum to get their hair done amounts to caring for their well-being. The abuse that underpins the everyday actions and comments is what stays closest to the surface of experience. Plus, it is normal for our subconscious mind to pay closer attention (and prioritise through the RAS) anything which threatens safety and increases risk. The rest gets filtered out.

Winning strategies

The reason I focus so fully on committing to a culture shift is because culture exists within the pores of an organisation, is embedded deep within every action and thought of every staff member and student. Policies and actions are disposable, are time bound and, metaphorically speaking, are more like the equipment in the gym than the mind-set required to get fit. You can point inspectors and parents to your frameworks and upload policy to your website, but without the commitment and intent to foster a culture steeped in mental wealth building practice and driven by a mission to put mental fitness above any other measure, it is nothing more than rubber stamping and posturing.

The intent in this step is to integrate throughout the school and the curriculum. I agree with this ambition. However, because there is a list of options to consider as part of that suggested integration, in my experience those are seen as just that – options for pick and mix – to play lip service to mental wealth building, rather than to integrate change across curriculum and culture. The words in the headlines are faultless in their intent, but many schools, pressured to do something (anything!) will pick the easy options and select a handful of changes to make, perhaps optimistically hoping that this will alter the culture or miraculously deliver integration. It won't.

Step 5: supporting staff

For me, beginning with staff (and yourself) is key to success in cementing any culture change and improving the mental well-being of an entire school. The very act of leaving them till last mitigates against any culture change strategy. There is no point trying to improve things for young people if staff retain a sense of being overlooked, undervalued or not cared for. It is an example of the metaphorical leaky bucket. You can keep pouring water in (in the form of policies, guidance, specialist staff to support students or mental health training for designated personnel), but that water will keep pouring out of the leaky hole created by overstretched, struggling staff. If anything, it will compound and worsen the situation, pouring oil on the fire of staff who feel pushed to the edge, underpaid, overworked or shoehorned into systems and procedures that do not allow them to practise the very teaching skills and passions they joined the profession to hone. How can you genuinely expect someone experiencing high levels of their own stress and anxiety, with work–life balance out of kilter, to be good at noticing the often subtle or even not so subtle signs of a young person struggling?

When we are in a state of chronic stress (as many working in secondary education sadly find themselves), we cannot over-ride the physiology of our brains and bodies that become thrust into persistent fight, flight or freeze. This process floods the brain and the body with adrenaline and cortisol. It clouds judgement, impairs clear thinking and deci-sion-making, limits capacity for focus and concentration and increases the likelihood of overwhelm and irritability. Followed to its logical conclusion, it leads to burnout, break-down, depression, even post-traumatic stress disorder (PTSD). This impacts individually and collectively. The school starts to experience increasing staff sickness and time off – one of the only forms of refuge and weapon in the armoury of a chronically stressed member of staff. The other is leaving, either for another school with a better culture or leaving the profession entirely. We all lose.

In short, make yourself and your staff the key priority for improving mental well build-ing and introducing repetitive tools of mental wealth building. Done well, it can be a matter of months before that improvement in staff mental well-being starts to cascade down to the student body. Staff will feel better equipped to spot students in need of help (based on their own experience) and they will feel better able to access their own creative,

Winning strategies

problem-solving mind in the pursuit of creative solutions for improving the well-being of everyone in the school. They will spot opportunities they hadn't previously seen for embedding mental wealth building into the normal curriculum. With the right encouragement (flowing from this positive culture), they will feel encouraged to get creative more often and to share their learning, expanding the flow of creative thinking through an upward spiral of growth. In short, the process of empowering staff through focusing on their mental well-being will enlarge their capacity for expansive thinking, and will lead to more innovative initiatives, and to greater productivity. Your school can transform from one merely getting by, hanging on by its metaphorical fingernails to the monitoring and measurement of academic grades and passes, to one which thrives and becomes an exemplar in the education arena, with other leaders flocking to understand what it is you have changed, and staff eager to join your team. Instead of stemming the growing tide of staff leaving, like the boy with his finger in the dyke, you acquire a new problem of a glut of applications for every vacant post. Those vacant posts happen less frequently too. The new problem becomes creating enough opportunities for career growth and expansion in a staff which is happy in its work. Yet, in this new culture you create, your continued focus on mental wealth building allows staff to apply their creative thinking to expanding their own skills and introducing projects that allow them to excel in their career.

Set a mental wealth strategy the lazy way

You know as well as I do that if there is one thing to get in the way of implementation or progress in any endeavour, it is the level of complexity or time involved. As a head teacher with wide-ranging and often conflicting demands on your time and your energy, this is even truer. So, the easier we make this, the more likely you are to implement. Quickly.

To be effective, it doesn't have to be complicated. When I work directly with clients on a one-to-one basis, I know that overwhelming them with a list of tasks or objectives and asking them for goals will not just hinder their progress, it will also bring it to a grinding halt. They will give up and return to the very habits or problems that brought them to me in the first place, tearing their hair out in frustration for not having moved forwards, feeling worse than when they started, because now they not only have the original problem, but they also have a sense of failure for having tried to solve the problem and 'failed'. They didn't fail. They just got challenged to take on too much too soon; or they tried to run before they could walk (all those clichés and metaphors exist for a good reason!). What they need instead is simplicity, tiny steps, movements so slight and imperceptible that they may not notice much progress as they make it, but as they reflect and look back, they see just how far they've come. Much like your Year 7 moving through the school. During the year, they seem much the same, with some marked shifts as they enter each new year group, but imagine the contrast in size and thinking by the time they reach Year 11. Your progress needs to be the same. Slowly, slowly catchy monkey – love those clichés.

Why, who, when, where, what, how?

When we're very busy, the easiest option can seem to just follow someone else's off-the-shelf, done for you plan. Sadly, mental wealth building doesn't work like this. The tools may be standardised but how you implement them to best effect for yourself and your

Winning strategies

school will be completely different from one organisation to the next. Because what lands well for one person in the telling or explanation, flies over another person's head. It's both what you do and how you understand and communicate what you do.

I read many articles and books on mental well-being from a variety of practitioners and standpoints – from the perspectives of neuroscience, neuropsychology, positive psychology, social psychology, occupational psychology, educational psychology, business leadership and neurolinguistic programming (NLP), to name just a few. Each will tell a version of the same set of events in our behaviour and our thinking, but each will tell it from a different perspective.

However, address these five basic tenets of any good journalist or public relations (PR) writer and you have a mental health strategy.

- **Why?**

  This was covered in the first few pages of the book. When any individual's mental wealth increases, their levels of concentration, focus, capacity for problem-solving and overall happiness increase. In other words, they perform better on *every* level!

  You perform better personally, as does every member of your teaching and support team, plus every student. Which means each person reaches a higher level of personal performance, and stands a far greater chance of being well equipped to progress beyond the school gates, in ways that are more fulfilling than a handful of crammed exam passes will ever deliver. Never mind the psychology or sociology. This is based on a simple truth of neuroscience. If every individual works to the optimum for their brain performance (homeostasis), they will achieve. Better than that, they stand a greater chance of achieving on their terms and are less likely to be swayed by the influence of others. You might think this could be a bad thing. After all, you want to influence the people in your school to take good decisions. However, that assumption of what a good decision is comes from a bias which suggests your version of good decisions aligns with another person's – and that there is some version of 'right' decisions. Whilst we might agree that it's important to learn respect for the law and the freedoms of others to the extent that physical or verbal abuse is unacceptable and to be discouraged, and each school will have its own standards of expected courtesies and behaviour, laying out some of those rules may cut across cultural and class boundaries in such a way that they become forms of institutional bias, verging on discrimination. Beyond that, do any of us have the right to determine what is right and what is wrong? Although we have commonality, this is a mistaken and ill-advised assumption, which potentially perpetuates cultural, gender and other forms of bias in ways you don't realise (because of the inherent bias in your own mind).

- **Who?**

  Everyone.

  The Anna Freud Centre provides lots of mechanisms and strategies for how you might do this, but, again, let's not overcomplicate it. Simply decide today to make it a part of the mission, the core vision, a part of every job description, a school rule, an induction letter to parents and pupils, a start of term whole-school assembly, an interview and recruitment induction activity/conversation, a daily morning registration activity.

  Instead of having a series of meetings with various groups to 'involve' people more or drawing up a policy in one go, start now, in this moment, to introduce small changes at each and every contact with every person in your school, so that behaviour change

Winning strategies

evolves and new, positive habits form. Policies, by their very nature are snapshots in time, rarely referred to as working documents and usually only used to cross-check for misdemeanours or mishaps in management or activities. Instead, when you set out to change today, having worked on your own mental well-being first (in order to access the full extent of your problem-solving, calm, creative mind), you will easily identify opportunities and find ways to capture and embed what works, whilst instantly recognising what doesn't. I can't overstate this. Don't overcomplicate!

Of course, you'll need someone to draw up a policy at some point in order to meet safeguarding, parental expectations and Ofsted requirements. Attend training and send others on training. However, don't wait until those elements are in place or rely on them for making the changes that will dramatically improve your own life and those of your students and staff. Begin the behaviour associated with positive mental well-being and mental wealth building that will lead you to a process that will determine your future policy. It's about tapping into your own social and commonsense skills as a human being first, a leader second.

- **When?**

    Now.

    There's no time for multiple meetings or policy planning, drafting and approval. Mental wealth building isn't like a project you plan to do at some later date. It's about how you live today, right now. Procrastination itself is, in fact, a feature of lower levels of mental wealth, of mental depreciation. As in Point 2, regarding who, you start today, in this very moment, but thinking about your own mental wealth and how you can increase your own personal stock of mental wealth. Mental wealth building is all about personal growth, personal responsibility, leadership by example, living according to your own values, discovering what those values are; and, by being one step ahead of the people you seek to enable in their own mental health growth, in writing their own personal success stories, you simply need to figure this out one step at a time, certain in the knowledge that there is no completion, no finished, perfect product, no end point. It is an infinite journey of growth, of learning. It is life itself. The richer your stock of mental wealth, the richer the stock of mental wealth of all those in your circle of influence. It truly is a social leveller, which has nothing to do with intellect, money, the street you were born on or the upbringing you had. It is all about you, entering on a quest like a crusader, to discover who you are, and inviting others to journey with you. Not to your destination, but to their destination. It is the joy of mental wealth building, as opposed to curriculum learning and examinations, that there is no single path, no correct answer, no right or wrong, no must try harder or could do better. It is the perfect learning journey where you, and everyone on the same path, head towards greater self-knowledge and the only comparison of any merit or meaning is the one you make with your own yesterday, last month, last year. If that sounds idealistic or utopian to the extent that the 'realist' or 'pragmatist' in you objects, then you are simply being managed by your own confirmation bias, prompted by your RAS. Take some time to reframe that particular story you tell yourself, and enable others to do the same. Let go of judgement. Open up to the joy that each and every person in your school and beyond has mental capacity and resources way beyond what they perhaps, or you, realise.

- **Where?**

    Here, with you.

    It's not a trick question. It's a prompt to remind you that it all starts with you, but once you introduce a different way of thinking and behaving about mental wealth

Winning strategies

building, there's no coming back. It creates an environment like the anthill or the beehive, in which every member knows their part and how to play it, even if you leave. Your legacy is a way of thinking and behaving, not a list of rules and procedures to follow. It is a gift that keeps on giving, if you forgive the cliché. Like Pandora's box, it's impossible to return to the past (unless every pupil and every member of staff within your leave of tenure also leave), but even in that case, the gift does not end for any of those who have benefitted from your influence and the steps you have taken to introduce real change in the way everyone thinks and feels about themselves and about their lives and their potential lives. They take it with them and it lives in them and with them.

- **What?**

  Throughout the book, there are suggestions, explanations, hints and clues as to what changes you can make. However, there is no should. Should is a word that dampens the very mental wealth thought processes that allow freedom of thought and expression that enhances resilience and positivity. The minute you couch something in 'should' it's like diluting the impact. Take any step or every step that has resonance and meaning for you. Because your education and experience to date may serve to resist this, I have included a section on suggestions for what to do when (and, of course, you can also access the resources of the Anna Freud Centre for a supportive, structured set of changes which can exist within familiar frameworks). However, working within familiar frameworks means you continue to do things in a similar way to the way you have always done them. You might be putting new clothes on the model, but the model remains the same. And we all know that other cliché – if you continue to do what you've always done, you will get what you've always got. You cannot fit Cinderella's slipper onto the ugly sister's foot just because you will it so, and then question why it doesn't work or, worse, use it as an 'I told you so' excuse for not succeeding. Nothing about improving mental wealth is complex. It merely requires commitment and an openness of mind. The question is, did you get to this point in the book, merely to rubbish or discredit the content, to troll any lack of specific steps via social media? Or have you retained an open mind to create the kind of change that you want for your school, and that the parents, students and staff want for themselves? And are you willing to fight your corner, if push comes to shove, confident in the knowledge that mentally wealthy minds are resilient, capable, achieving, resourceful, happy minds?

- **How?**

  Start with you.
  - Get your personal mental health in order.
  - Let go of any story you tell yourself about what isn't possible for you, or others, or what you can or can't do.
  - Lead before delegating.
  - Start with actions that evolve into policies by documenting learning as you go.
  - With each step you make forwards, share insights and learning with staff, pupils and parents.
  - Take one tiny step at a time. It will soon amount to miles, but don't try to rush or force anyone or anything, including yourself.
  - Set a huge 5-year goal, and tiny daily goals that journey towards it.
  - Remain committed and consistent.
  - This is not a to-do list, it's a journey.

Winning strategies

In short, allow your strategic development for the greater mental health of the school to evolve from your own journey of self-development. That way, you will always remain committed and always commit to improvement, and will enjoy a seamless connection between the greater achievements of yourself, your students, your staff and the whole school. This is what holistic mental wealth planning looks like and how it works.

Beyond that, here's some tools and insights that will inform your progress. Remember that each tool, suggestion and insight is one you can apply both for yourself, and implement within classes and staff meetings, training and even (especially) in day-to-day conversations as part of your wider leadership strategy.

Make insignificant changes

Small hinges swing big doors. I learned this phrase a while ago from an American business coach. At the time, it didn't make a whole lot of sense, but gradually I figured it out. I use this style of thinking a lot with clients.

The smallest, seemingly insignificant changes can lead to the biggest outcomes. And people are nearly always surprised by how dramatic effects can occur from the tiniest shift – in thinking and behaviour. Think Rosa Parkes if you want a perfect example.

So I ask you to suspend cynicism or judgement here and trust in yourself – and the process. Above all, trust in yourself. So often I have seen the look of mild disbelief that small changes I am suggesting will make a bigger impact than believed possible. Especially when it relates to other people and their responses. 'X person won't go along with that'. I never fail to be amazed at the changes that can and do occur – no matter how often I witness or hear it. This is where the magic happens.

What kind of small things, you might well ask?

I'll furnish you with suggestions to get the ball rolling, but as you may have figured, there is no single magic formula (even though this *is* where the magic happens). It's down to you and your exceptionally talented students and colleagues to assist here. (And your students and colleagues *will* amaze you if you just give them the opportunity. Create an environment of trust, no-blame and freedom to experiment, and watch the magic happen.)

Throw pebbles

Welcome every student and every member of staff by name, every day.

Get teachers to do the same at the classroom door – welcoming students before the class begins. A 2018 study[9] encouraging positive greetings at the door (PGD) within a middle school setting showed that such a strategy 'produced significant improvements in academic engaged time and reductions in disruptive behaviour. Moreover, results from a social validity questionnaire indicated that teachers found the PGD strategy to be feasible, reasonable, and acceptable'.

In relation to mental fitness, who doesn't feel better when they're acknowledged? In the vulnerable adolescent years, this might prove to be even more powerful. Just don't expect them to act like they welcome it! They need to retain their 'cool' after all.

Here's an extract from Edutopia,[10] who reported on the research:

In the study, when teachers started class by welcoming students at the door, academic engagement increased by 20 percentage points and disruptive behavior decreased by

Winning strategies

9 percentage points –potentially adding 'an additional hour of engagement over the course of a five-hour instructional day'.

Ten middle school teachers were randomly assigned by the researchers to one of two groups. The first group started class by greeting their students at the door, saying each student's name while using a nonverbal greeting such as a handshake or nod. The teachers also used pre-corrective statements – reminders of what to do at the start of class like, 'Spend the next few minutes reviewing what we covered yesterday'. If a student had struggled with their behavior the previous day, the teachers often gave a positive message to encourage them to improve.

Teachers in the second group attended classroom management training sessions offered by their schools, but they weren't given any specific instructions on how to start class. Researchers observed classrooms in the fall and spring, looking at academic engagement – how attentive students were to their teacher or classwork – and disruptive behavior, including speaking out of turn, leaving one's seat, and distracting classmates. Both measures improved in classrooms where teachers greeted their students, confirming what many teachers already know: Meeting students' emotional needs is just as important as meeting their academic needs.

The results from this study suggest that teachers who spend time on the front end to implement strategies such as the positive greetings at the door will eventually save more time on the back end by spending less time reacting to problem behaviour and more time on instruction.

It's too easy to get caught up in sharing the problems of budgetary shortfalls, staff and pupil absence, Ofsted inspections, pupil behaviour issues and targets, to name a few of the hot topics 'trending' on social media channels. You might think this is pragmatic – and unavoidable. However, continual focus on 'problem' issues only fosters more problems.

Instead, drawing on solution-focused practise, start to inculcate a climate of positivity throughout the whole school with a 'what's been good?' start to every school day and every staff meeting.

Practise gratitude

The difficulty with so many highly effective tactics and strategies for improved mental health is that they sound too easy. Which means they are also too easy to give up on too soon, or to implement half-heartedly, to look for something more substantial, perhaps.

Gratitude journals are one such example. I confess that I was one of those people who took on that kind of flippant approach (that also came from failing to embrace the 'empty your cup' philosophy) to my own mental well-being. In all honesty, I didn't really 'get it'. I tried (or so I thought) to embrace gratitude, being thankful for my home, the roof over my head, the food on my table (you know the kind of thing), and I would, occasionally, compile lists of things I was grateful for, combining them into a journal, which wasn't really a journal, more of a notebook I took to writing personal development notes in from time to time. Unsurprisingly, it didn't do much for me. I didn't feel better. In fact, I didn't feel different at all. And that was where the real key was. It was right under my nose, but it took me a while to see it and understand it in a slow building series of eureka moments.

The examples I included – and that you might be tempted to include too – were very generic, not terribly personal to me. They were, arguably, key fundamentals to be

Winning strategies

grateful for. Extremely grateful. But they weren't things I was really connecting to on any deeply felt level. I was making the mistake of thinking gratitude, rather than feeling gratitude.

To be practised effectively, it's best to combine with what I describe as insignificant moments of joy or quick wins. In other words, you need to pay closer attention to the world around you, how it impacts on you and your role in it. For example, you might practise some self-congratulation on a quick win, such as tapping into empathy when faced with a highly disgruntled parent and generating an atmosphere of calm and resolution. You could journal that quick win and, in the writing of it, re-experience the good feelings associated with the achievement, adding your sense of gratitude as the cherry on the top. If you set up a practice of doing this, perhaps at the end of each day for 15 minutes, choosing to find three quick wins within your day, you start to build your own stock of mental wealth, enhanced resilience and greater positivity.

Once you master this for yourself, your creative mind is more fully engaged and you begin to see the potential for introducing this as a tool for implementation for your staff and within the school day for students. For example, 5 minutes of assembly time could, arguably, be used more productively (in the long term) on completing just such a journal. However, it isn't for me to tell you precisely how to implement this. Each school and each head teacher has different ways of working – and it is not for me to tell you which way is best. It is something best learned when you work it through as a whole school – and learn as you go what works best and how best to assimilate it into school culture.

The role of decision-making

Since this is a book about mental health leadership, it would be wrong to exclude some of the challenges that relate purely to being a good leader, one who makes good decisions in the best interests of the school and the wider context of community and society. There's no doubt your intention as a leader would be to meet each of those demands and to do it well. Sadly, many people who enter leadership roles are provided with no special training (at least no more than an occasional day of training here and there). Yet, good leadership is transformational. We only have to think of leaders we admire and it will never be for their command of data, or their report writing skill, or even for their great policies (unless the impact of those policies is so huge and transformational they can't be ignored, like creating the NHS, for example). Instead, great leadership, whoever you most admire, is a mark of someone adept in communicating an idea so powerfully that others cannot fail to be persuaded of its relative merits – or demerits – and are driven to take action towards supporting the furtherance of that idea. Training can be a little thin on the ground in all walks of life, but maybe more so in education. In short, you are a great leader if people choose to follow you, not if they are mandated to. It can be a lonely path, where your only trustworthy counsel may be your own conscience.

An understanding of ways in which you might increase your own power and confidence in that counsel would, presumably, be welcome. Good decision-making that supports your position as a leader and the ideas you choose to propagate can only help you in this. However, as I've alluded to throughout the pages of this book, you will be hampered in the quality of your decision-making if your own mental wealth is not in good order. Overwhelm and stress contribute to self-doubt, loss of concentration and, in turn, to decision-making which is confused, unreliable and unwittingly makes situations, including performance and the wider mental fitness of the school, worse rather

89

better. You can see how impactful this might be when you consider that we make 35,000 decisions per day on average.[11]

I hope you are beginning to appreciate that every aspect of your life is intricately interwoven with your personal mental well-being and, since you do not live in a vacuum, your own mental well-being will impact on every one of the people in your sphere of influence, to a lesser or greater degree (which, ironically, is also dependent on their own state of mental well-being). Mental well-being is a circular flow throughout families and communities and society. It is not a compartmentalised state of being which is – or can be – cut off from the world around us. Which is why I am so keen to emphasise that it is vital you start with you.

Change the dialogue from what to who

One of the fundamental errors that impacts negatively on young people for the long term (unwittingly and innocently) is the repetitive mantra relating to questioning *what* outcomes they want and suggesting *what* outcomes they can expect. For the large part, we (parents and teachers) tell them *what* to expect and *what* to want (even when we think we don't) and we repeatedly ask them *what* they want to achieve, *what* job or career they want to follow, *what* kind of courses they want to take, *what* university they want to go to, *what* kind of life they want for themselves. All the while, we are manipulating their belief systems about what is possible for them, making a judgement call about them and their potential and suggesting a certainty of outcomes based on our own confirmation bias. The intention is always to raise their aspirations, but what we intend and what we achieve are two entirely different things. The tragedy is that the modern education system and a child's success within it remain almost wholly within the hands of a single teacher who resonates, who 'gets' a child, who manages to find the key that sparks their enthusiasm and their passion. And that is the key.

If, instead of creating a culture where we explicitly and implicitly ask *what* they want and *what* they want to be, we ask *who* they want to be. This sparks a whole new way of thinking and initiates a process of potential and possibility. It ignites a passion, an interest, and is a direct arrow into the heart of *who* they really are. Even if they can't initially answer the question of *who* they are and *what* matters most to them, if we encourage them to think of *who* they want to be, we can change everything. And this works no matter how late in the day we ask the question. The only obstacle to the effectiveness of such a strategy that changes the very culture and challenges underpinning beliefs around what education is and what it does, is that, unless a child feels safe to express their own thoughts or values, they will still tell you what they think you – or their parents or key figures in their life – expect them to say. This is because they may already have created their own internal filter that says expressing what they really think is unacceptable or that it is not possible, therefore not worth sharing. Their primitive unconscious mind seeks to invalidate what they really feel because previous experience (for example, being told to be realistic, to grow up, being laughed at or ridiculed, not taken seriously) makes such an admission or expression of desire a dangerous strategy. To maintain self-preservation, to keep them safe, to protect their very being, their first knee-jerk response will be the familiar, 'dunno'. Do not challenge this head on. Instead, persist through a shift in leadership and teaching style to encourage every student to continue to wonder about *who* they want to become. Ideally, this is based on *who* they admire, so can be integral to teaching, woven, for example, into history or English or music or sport. As this becomes a familiar style of working and questioning, with examples and case studies from your own and staff or guest speaker lives (which is a key reason why making sure your own mental fitness house is in order first is so important!), you can encourage an expansion of thinking from a specific person to a why this person, what is it about them, is it the qualities they seem to have, is it what they have achieved, is it something else? Keep encouraging them to dive deeper in their own thinking and, ideally, to express this in writing or in visual or musical terms, to expand and embed their thinking more fully. Remember that it doesn't have to be someone famous. It's probably better if it isn't. It can be someone else in their lives, a family member, a friend, a sporting coach, another parent, a teacher, anyone!

Once they have a sense of *who* and begin unpicking *why*, then you can help them begin to connect to *what*. The critical aspect of this is for you and your staff to suspend all value judgement about whether you think this is reasonable, viable, possible or doable. That is not your call and, as the testimony of many a famous and not so famous person will tell you, you will be wrong unless you insist that you are right! In other words, if they acquiesce to your professional expertise as a teacher or your status as a respected adult, if they are more keen to please and 'do the right' thing, then you will undoubtedly condemn them to your vision of their future, rather than their own. If, however, you encourage them to figure out what steps they need to take to reverse engineer their sense of *who* they want to be, to begin to think of it as a plan to create a possible future, then you will be helping them to (a) have confidence in their decisions and their choices; (b) think something through beyond a surface level; (c) have increased awareness of themselves and what they want; and (d) have the courage and wherewithal to change their decision at some point along the journey and know how to self-correct to a new path, should that become their choice.

Our role, as parents and educators, is surely to enable reasoned thinking, choice and self-determination, so that young people stand the very best chance of achieving their potential. More than that, the future of this planet depends on them being the kind of creative problem-solvers and action takers who can come up with workable global solutions. We are no longer in the world of factories, mass production, typing pools and homogeneous work practices. As human beings, as contributors to society and as workers, we are required to bring more of ourselves, our unique skills and innovative thought processes. If Covid-19 has demonstrated anything, it is the demand for highly adaptable, smart, creative, can-do people who believe anything is possible until it is.

Through this way of working, you help young people fulfil their own potential and you increase and improve the skill sets of a workforce which requires innovation, disruption, possibility, daring and courage.

Belonging and identity

I doubt there exists a school without the intention of fostering belonging. The challenge is with mastering the art of building a sense of belonging at the same time as being inclusive. No amount of exam passes or top grades will create a sense of belonging if a child already feels like an outsider on some level, such as gender, race, income, accent, class, disability. It is why young people become so vulnerable to gangs and sexual grooming. Those with mal-intent have no trouble grasping the young person's need to feel that sense of belonging, through showing an interest, providing friendship, understanding and empathy. Why is it that we persist in institutional-style responses? Time? Fatigue? Overwork? Probably all of

Winning strategies

these. However, each of these are, in part, stories we tell ourselves of situations we cannot change and so we set the standard of impotence, powerlessness, victimhood. Again, it is why I repeatedly chant the mantra throughout the pages of this book that change has to start with you. You need to reframe your own sense of self and what's possible, and stop behaving as if you have no power, that you are a victim – of government policy, of Ofsted, of parent demands. Demonstrate to others that it is possible to make a difference against the odds by standing with integrity and authenticity for what you believe in. If you don't, what chance have your students got? Honestly.

Behaviour and identity

There is a tendency towards fixation on behaviour within school. To some extent, this is wholly justified. However, without clear boundaries around the extent of that behavioural conformity, it becomes a constricting, disempowering, disabling tool that robs young people of their identity and their courage to feel that who they are is acceptable. Teaching good behaviour should not be the same as teaching conformity, robbing people of their individuality and the courage to be themselves. When we rob people of their individuality, and implicitly or explicitly suggest that their unique qualities are in some way unacceptable, we risk a foundation for mental ill health at worst, and low confidence or endemic self-doubt at best.

The child shut down for expressing its individuality, is more likely to become the adult who shies away from standing out and stepping up to lead…. Leading would come at an inner emotional cost as the fear of rejection… is amplified by decades of reinforcing the notion that blending in with the crowd is the only way to stay safe.

The biggest triggers for us picking us picking up new masks or armour is shame. Shame is essentially guilt made personal. 'We feel bad about something and, instead of remembering it was just a behaviour, something we did, we conflate that self-criticism as being about who we *are*'.[12]

The kind of trigger referred to above, in Clare Josa's excellent book on imposter syndrome, can occur, of course, outside of school and in the home. Which is why it is doubly important to cultivate a powerful environment of personal reinforcement, of expanding individuality and self-belief both within the classroom and in the playground.

It is worth questioning, therefore, the boundaries of, for example, school uniform rules that relate, for example, to hairstyles or footwear. As with anything relating to building mental wealth, there is no one-size-fits-all policy or directive that I can recommend you adopt and adhere to in order to ensure the mental fitness of *every* member of staff and every pupil. However, it is vital that you create freedom within some of the rules for exceptions and case-by-case decisions. It may seem to be an added burden to already overburdened workloads. After all, blanket rules seem so much easier to enforce. But that's just it, enforcement is the bedfellow of conformity. Creativity, empowerment and personal fulfilment do not come from a place of conformity. It needs to be made very clear and explicit to each pupil the difference between rules for safety and respect and rules which impinge on liberty and the right to freedom of expression. There is a need to respect authority, but subtlety of expression is also critical. Young people can tend to see things in black and white, right and wrong, always and never – and our desire, as adults, to reinforce this contributes to a fixed mindset. A fixed mindset is the bedrock of future identity issues. It forces young people to define who they are by what they do, to globalising a simple behaviour and

92

creating all-or-nothing thinking, such as 'I'll never be able to do that' and 'People like me never succeed'. These are hardly ways of thinking you want in your school, because they are non-conducive to growth or learning or commitment to learning or to any kind of belief in potential. For children caught in the performance gap, they remain there and resolutely so.

Unless they rebel completely. In order to retain their identity, which they realise at a subconscious level is being eroded, they may resist all rules and all norms of behaviour, but potentially at the cost of the very help they might need in terms of learning or inclusion. Greater rules of enforcement or penalties are not the solution.

Strong anti-bullying policies play their part in nurturing belonging and, thereby, strengthening self-belief. However, never assume that because someone performs well, behaves impeccably, 'fits in', that they really feel like they fit in. It starts with fostering self-belief, instead of self-doubt. In my own case, though easily qualifying for a good girls grammar school (1970s) and being good at playing the game of fitting in by wearing the full uniform, abiding by the rules, showing up every day on time, never causing any disruption or problems, this masked the fact that I never overcame the belief that I was stupid, which I acquired from older brothers and the belief that only those with status and money would ever achieve much. I became one of the many invisible children, who was overlooked (didn't stand out enough) and not encouraged to do anything at all, other than pass my exams, with which I duly complied.

Mindful language

People pontificate regularly on mindfulness. It has almost become the buzzword of the early 21st century. However, rarely do people have any real sense of what this means or how they might effectively apply it on a moment-by-moment basis within their thinking and behaviour. Nevertheless, language use is the perfect place to practise mindfulness and foster positive habits around use of language.

One of the keys to reinforcing either a growth or a fixed mindset and associated identity issues (e.g. I am a bad person v I behaved badly towards my teacher/fellow student) is our use of language. It is too easy to be careless in our use of language (including body language and facial expressions), especially when we are under pressure, tired, overworked, overwhelmed, all typical laments of the teaching fraternity. However, as expressed in almost every line of this book, when you take care of your own mental well-being first – (remember the aircraft oxygen mask analogy, which requires you to place your own mask over your face before helping another) – you can operate from a place of clarity and calm. Mindfulness is a beautifully reinforcing behaviour, in that, whilst we can only apply it once we attain a relative state of calm, once we practise it, we support the maintenance and reinforcement of the very state of calm we entered in the first place. I include body language, because young people remain acutely sensitive to the interpretation of facial expression and the use of language to decipher the meaning that is intended to be conveyed. In every moment, the brain uses every sensory input to create a rich and textural assessment of a situation, event, person or moment. It will also pay closest attention to anything novel or suggestive of a risk to personal safety and attach greater importance to these elements. I describe this as pattern matching. All brains do it, laying down patterns of information for the future, which define how you behave in any given situation.

Young people, of course, are laying down many more fresh patterns of thinking and behaviour than an adult each day, so are more acutely aware of nuances of tone and expression

Winning strategies

than an adult might be, adding their own interpretation of what that means along the way. You will be aware that we do not stop doing this as adults, but it is more frequent in young people. The patterns that get laid down become our new 'truths' of the world. The meaning we construe in our youthful mind risks becoming the truth of our adult world.

There are so many examples you will recognise throughout your day and, probably, in your own behaviour. For example, 'John, why is it you always seem to be late?' spoken with a disapproving tone and facial expression, which triggers John's primitive mind, driven to keep him safe from perceived danger with fight, flight or freeze behaviour. John's inner processing may interpret this as, 'Ms Osaka hates me. She's always hated me. All figures of authority hate me. I need to resist this or I will die'. This thinking results in disruptive, rebellious behaviour, characterised by frequent anger and irritability. Do not make the mistake of thinking this is simply poor behaviour which needs to be controlled. This is a behaviour associated with mental wealth depletion (the fight part of fight, flight, freeze) and, as such, requires the same supportive and enabling response given to a child who is anxious, fearful or sad. Or 'I must be a really bad person. She is right. I am always late. I can never change. I am always wrong. I always let people down. I must become invisible or I will die'. This thinking results in passive, self-denigrating behaviour. Such a person may be easier to 'handle'. They will be polite, conform quickly to any request for changes in behaviour, but they set up a negative internal dialogue that can escalate self-doubt and lead to depression or anxiety.

Instead, adopt a different approach. Be mindful of your tone, facial expression and body language. Here's a way you might handle this particular situation differently. It involves, empathy and an explicit and expansive explanation of just *why* it matters, not just to you, but to them.

Explain why it's important to be on time with examples that relate in some way to the student's own experience. This gives them an opportunity to make sense of the request/demand because it gives them an opportunity to empathise. Few children or young people will happily act on a request or instruction without understanding why it matters. You might also explain how you – or their teacher or, better still, their peers – might be negatively impacted by lateness. Explain how we are all human and how sometimes we can't help being late. Perhaps share an example from your own experience. Shared vulnerability is powerful (you might demonstrate you are a human being with failings just like them!). Share an example from a fictitious child (with a potentially similar personality or life experience to the child you are speaking to) of how there might be a good reason for being late, but how they could seek help for that to prevent it causing the kinds of problems you've already described. This gives them an opportunity to either share something they haven't already shared, or to feel heard and understood and to contemplate alternative ways of dealing with the situation in the future.

This might seem a time-consuming approach, but it will save you time and grief in the long run, will improve your own reasoning, communication and empathy skills, will demonstrate those skills to them and may head off a mental health or personal crisis down the line. It's worth it on every level.

Focus on what works

Focusing on problems only expands the problems. (Remember the section on the RAS, in which we explained how the brain seeks out confirmation of existing patterns of belief, creating a confirmation bias.)

Winning strategies

The brain enjoys seeking out similarity, engaging in pattern matching. So when we focus on what isn't working, what feels bad, what causes disruption, then our natural neurology receives this as an indicator to seek out (and expect) more of the same – similar problems, other things that feel bad, don't work, cause disruption. Again, traditional logic might argue that there is value in this seeking out, for example, schools or heads with similar problems – or Googling the problems for potential solutions does, indeed, sometimes seem to work when we stumble across a solution that someone else has discovered.

However, more often than not, it just creates a deepening of the problems. Now your neurology is feeding off mirror neurons. Mirror neurons in the brain create emotional contagion; and in this example, the contagion stems from other people's helplessness or struggles, other people's problems. Even though you may believe you draw comfort from this. After all, you're no longer alone with the problem, other people share your concerns, your worries and your challenges. There's comfort in community and belonging – even when that community is filled with negative energy. (See how easily this innate behaviour reflects the challenges of your students growing up in negative environments.) However, there is a risk that what you create is an unofficial members club of worry, problems and angst. We see this amplified on social media. Where there is indeed much sharing of best practice, the material that really spreads like wildfire and is duplicated over and over, is the whinging and whining about the problems faced within the sector. In effect, a negativity bias is being nurtured and well fed.

The more you think about something, the more likely it is to occur (or to re-occur), so surrounding yourself and your colleagues with thoughts and words around problems increases the likelihood that those problems will perpetuate. Sounds illogical, but the social psychology provides us with evidence. 'The more familiar a scenario is – the more images of it that we've seen or imagined – the more likely it seems'.[13] In effect, we are building a negativity bias.

The good news is that social psychologists have identified a positivity ratio of 5:1. This means, in short, that to create a healthy balance for yourself (and your school community), you need to work towards outweighing each 'bad' or negative experience with five 'good' or positive experiences.

Which brings me back to those pebbles in the pond, insignificant changes and small hinges swinging big doors.

Fostering a culture where students and staff alike are required to share 'what's been good' helps tip the positivity ratio. As you pay closer attention to the small things that work, that feel good, you not only tip the balance in favour of general positivity, you massively amplify the effect by firing up mirror neurons, enabling others to feed on this positive energy. This strategy comes from solution-focused brief therapy.

What else tips it?

Challenging yourself and others to repeatedly define their days, and indeed, each meeting and lesson with thinking driven by, for example, 'what do I want from this, what would make it better, what works well?'. Getting people to express those thoughts ensures they embed the practice – and feed that positivity ratio.

It stimulates creativity, innovation, commitment and focus. Again, thinking of mirror neurons, if you foster this kind of culture and energy within the staff and governors, you amplify the impact on the student body too. Mirror neurons are powerful – and key – when it comes to learning from observing.

Winning strategies

'Thanks to mirror neurons the emotions we portray have a direct influence on others. This is why teachers have to make the effort to control their emotions, avoid teacher burnout, in order to use mirror neurons as an asset'.[14] So, a simple shift in the process of your interactions with staff and pupils and the language used, can create a seismic shift in whole-school well-being.

It's important also to note that highly sensitive people, which might describe many adolescents struggling with mental health issues or stress, are particularly susceptible to the impact of mirror neurons, good or bad.

Solution-focused practice

As I learned early in my study of solution-focused brief therapy, it is simple, but not easy. Mastering a more conscious, solution-focused way of speaking, questioning and behaving, so that it becomes endemic practice within the school, can feel difficult and slow going to begin with. It is so easy to slip back into traditional ways of thinking and behaving the moment the first 'crisis' occurs.

This is no reason to deter you from making this a key priority in your whole-school mental health strategy. Its effective implementation positively impacts on goal setting, performance and achievement for individuals and the whole school, as well as contributing to greater levels of mental fitness. If you do what you've always done, you'll get what you've always got. And you didn't pick up this book to keep things the same.

Also, giving up because it's hard isn't a permissible attitude for your students, so don't allow it to be one for you, your governors or your staff. If there was ever an appropriate place to instil discipline and enforce simple rules, this would be it.

I'll let you into a secret

When I first learned this style of working at the beginning of a course in solution-focused brief therapy, I hated it. I resisted it like the plague, found it difficult and it challenged me on so many levels. I had achieved a comfortable and, I thought, successful way of working with clients. The change temporarily impacted on my confidence with those clients and made me feel like a complete novice again. I suddenly felt incompetent. It seemed bad for business and bad for me – and because I wasn't very accomplished at this new skill, my clients just looked confused when I tried introducing questions like, 'what's been good?' or 'when you wake tomorrow, if a miracle had happened overnight, what would be the first thing you would notice that would be different?'. My lack of confidence fed their confusion and I didn't know how to adapt my questioning to help them find the solutions they needed to their mental health challenges.

Every fibre of my being wanted to throw in the towel and to go back to what I knew best.

Fortunately, a very good friend and colleague, who had taken the training with me, not only shared her own similar feelings, but also gave me a few other questions I could ask that felt more comfortable for me, like, 'Can you list 10 of your positive qualities?'. That may not seem like an easier question to you – or even relevant to your situation in school (on the other hand it might be) – but it allowed me to break through my resistance. My clients started responding positively, and they started to achieve more, without much need on my part to come up with strategies for them. They just began to find their own way and discover the best solutions for themselves. Which was exactly the point.

96

Eventually, I gained a level of mastery which increased my confidence and changed the balance of therapy sessions completely. I went from being the one doing most of the talking, to being the one doing most of the listening. My clients were working things out for themselves; and feeling all the better for it. They were also achieving greater success in life – in relationships and in work.

In fact, I became so familiar with conducting conversations in this way that something quite remarkable happened as a result. I tell you this only to demonstrate the impact of pebbles in ponds and small hinges swinging big doors.

One evening, a group of contractors who worked in the NHS Trust I was also employed by as a senior manager, organised a small social gathering to which I was invited. I sat next to a man with whom I'd had limited professional dealings. However, we got into a conversation where he asked about my hypnotherapy and I asked about his life and family. He told me he was commuting each week from Belfast and only got to see his family at the weekends. He also told me how he missed his family, would dearly love to spend more time with them and do more of the things he used to love. He knew this would also help him get fit and lose weight, but couldn't commit to any of this because he could never get to training or make any guarantees about his weekends. He was at the beck and call of his work and resigned to it.

I honestly don't remember the exact things I said to him, but I am sure I naturally asked him solution-focused questions which helped him access his own resources. We said goodbye and that was that, a pleasant evening spent with pleasant people.

It was the last I saw or heard of him, until about 1 year later when a message popped into my LinkedIn inbox. I was shocked and amazed. Here's what it said:

> Hi Shirley, I am just writing to let you know that you started a series of events by telling me to 'just do it'. I am now back in Belfast working in partnership with a great guy... Since February, we have been helping companies and organisations get through the current downturn. I am home with my family, taking an active role and also losing weight, nearly 20 kg since February.

I tell this story only to highlight the monumental shifts that can occur from a few suitably posed questions. Imagine what can be achieved when a whole-school culture shifts even a small way in an equally positive direction!

Do you think that might just make a difference to the mental fitness, and achievement, of your staff and students too? I think so.

You have to be willing to go back a few steps, to lose a little sure-footedness for a short while, as you gather expertise and confidence, but share with your staff what you are doing and why. Bring them with you. Stumble together. Get it wrong sometimes before you begin to reap the rewards. You might need to take a step back before you take three steps forwards.

Ask a miracle question

Here's an example of a miracle question:

> On a scale of 0 to 10, you tell me you're on a 5. Imagine the rest of your day was the same as normal and you went to bed. Eventually, you fall asleep and a miracle happens. You don't know the miracle has happened until the next day, when you

Winning strategies

> wake. What do you notice that's different, that tells you you're no longer a 5, but a 6 on the scale?

or a simpler version, 'If the problem miraculously evaporated, what would I/you do instead or do differently?'. If you practise asking miracle questions, either internally of yourself or externally of another, you will get closer to achieving workable solutions, a positive mindset and greater peace of mind. You will do so more quickly than you ever imagined. If you want to know more – and learn how to practise this expertly – watch Insoo Kim Berg.[15]

Avoid telling yourself or others to *not* do something or to *stop* doing something

When considering any perceived or identified problem, you might reasonably ask the question, 'What would make it better?'.

However, in order to answer that question effectively and start coming up with reasonable solution-focused responses, your first challenge is to avoid responses relating to what you don't want and what you want to stop.

Remember that stress, anxiety, low mood and anger (exemplified in your school by irritability, poor behaviour or lack of engagement, for example) are all feelings, not actions. They are also feelings we do not enjoy. (Yes, it's true that some people believe they thrive on stress, but the cortisol and adrenaline regularly running around their brain and body is telling a different story of impending health disaster, because it increases the risk of stroke and heart attack. At some point down the line, you will pay for the stress you experience in the present.)

So, in answer to the original question, 'how could it be better?', a common response might be couched in terms of feelings that you want to stop having or things you want to stop happening, e.g. 'I'd be less anxious' or 'I'd worry less' or 'we wouldn't have an Ofsted inspection' or 'our Ofsted grading would be better'.

This leaves people in a disempowered state. Problems perceived or described in this way keep the person stuck, to the extent that the only 'solution' they frequently come up with is to move away from the problem. Which, in the case of teachers, means leaving their jobs. In the case of students, it might mean changing schools, becoming sick or provoking exclusion. (Yes, consciously or unconsciously, a student under stress may find exclusion the path of least resistance when it comes to feeling better about themselves or their situation.)

Both answers keep the mind focused on the problem of worry and anxiety, and present no options for how a solution might be framed. The only apparent solution springing to mind immediately can be to escape the situation.

In fact, some GPs, when consulted with problems of low mood, stress at work or anxiety, can recommend just such a course of action. They can't be blamed for this. For their part, they may not have adequate resources to recommend suitable therapies; and they don't want to unnecessarily prescribe antidepressants and beta blockers, when they perceive the problem as situational, rather than internal.

The idea of 'not' doing something is what I describe as a logical, rational construct. I might have a logical sense of what I mean by not worrying, but what does not worrying actually mean? What alternatives are presented as potential solutions to a problem if we define it in 'not doing' terms? For example, if I am not paragliding or planning to

Winning strategies

go paragliding, does that give you any clue as to what I am actually doing or planning to do?

No. By contrast, it focuses the mind on the very thing you say you are not doing or don't want to be doing.

So saying or thinking about not worrying actually makes us worry more and brings us no closer to a solution. Let me explain. Imagine you are on the phone to a friend and you ask them what they are doing later that day. Suppose they answer that they will not be skiing, or they will not be watching TV, or they will not be playing football, not painting a picture, not knitting a jumper.

Do any of those answers illuminate your understanding of what they will actually be doing? No.

Do all of those answers conjure up an image or impression of what they won't be doing? Yes.

This means your mind is now focused more fully on what the person is not doing, yet you still have no idea what the person will actually be doing.

It's exactly like those examples you have probably heard when someone asks you not to imagine pink elephants. The moment they do this, all you can imagine is pink elephants.

All those words used to describe an act of not doing something prompt the rich and vast complexity of your brain to make connections with everything you've ever heard, seen and experienced in the past, to source examples of similar things you remember. A single word, sound or image will fire a series of neural connections that bring to mind something that relates to it.

Your mind does this, unconsciously, in every waking moment. We depend upon it to do so, in order to make sense of the world and create shortcuts to learning and progress. In effect, it is constantly refining and developing its own personal shorthand, a sensory description of everything you see, do, taste, touch, hear, experience.

So, focusing on what we don't want means our neural networks continue firing to present us with examples of similar experiences. We're effectively giving the brain an instruction to do so. Which means we worry more, and start thinking about other situations or events that make us feel equally bad, fed up – or whatever the original problem feeling was. Which also means we lose focus and increase overwhelm.

Any children in your school lack focus and experience overwhelm? Indeed.

You can help by encouraging them to think and talk more frequently about what they want instead. Put simply, if you don't want to feel stressed and worried, you might want to feel calm and confident, for example.

Warning: the more anxious, low or stressed the individual is, the harder this will be for them. They may be reluctant or seem uncooperative. Be patient, be creative and help them, gently teasing out small differences that might be better.

But beware offering your own version of what *you* think is better. This could just sink them further into the mire, because they may feel they cannot live up to that, thereby increasing their stressed response.

Challenging Eeyore thinking

Example: If I ask you what would make planning your curriculum easier, and you answer something along the lines of 'not having to conform to the changing demands of Ofsted', or phrased differently, 'being free from the changing demands of Ofsted', the

Winning strategies

instruction you give to your brain is to think about the changing demands of Ofsted. Which probably leads to greater stress. It certainly doesn't lead directly to ways you could plan a better curriculum. This single example is a clear example of how you – and by association, your school culture – are fostering anxiety with Eeyore thinking.[16]

Here's a few examples of anxiety-driven responses:

Q. What would make it better?

- not having to fill in these endless spreadsheets
- not having Ofsted breathing down my neck

Moving thought processes stuck in negativity requires follow-up questions that focus on what you would do instead.

Here's a couple of example follow-up questions to the preceding answers:

- If you didn't have to complete those endless spreadsheets, what would you do instead?
- If you didn't have Ofsted breathing down your neck, what would you do differently?

When you – or the people around you – are immersed in a negative space, they may not see the point of these follow-up questions. Negativity can be disguised in many people's minds as reality or pragmatism. They will rationalise that these are things they cannot change. Yet, these are victim-driven, disempowered responses, that feed the downward spiral of more disempowered and negative thinking. Think of Eeyore in Winnie the Pooh, 'Wish I could say yes, but I can't'.[17]

Remember, if you want a different outcome, you have to do things differently. And doing things differently has to start by thinking things differently.

It's easy to hide behind excuses and blame other people, especially disembodied ones who come in the form of statutory guidelines or performance targets.

This thinking may be something you recognise in yourself. Or in others. Or both. Whichever way, it requires gentle challenging and persistent self-coaching to achieve desired changes.

The first step may simply be observation of it happening. Be mindful of the thoughts or language you use. Start by simply noticing it. Once you notice it, you have created a metaphorical opening, a space for alternative and more productive thoughts to creep in.

Having noticed the 'what I *wouldn't* be doing' thinking or speech patterns, you now allow yourself to become curious. This part, in theory, should be easy for you, as a teacher. Your very profession is driven by a passion for learning, which starts with curiosity. This process provides the perfect opportunity to reignite your passion for learning and for growth.

Having become curious, consider alternative responses: 'If I wasn't doing this, what would I be doing instead? If I didn't have to do this, what would I do instead? If I wasn't under pressure, how would I manage this instead?'. You get the picture.

If you struggle with powerful inner resistance to this preceding step in the process, or can't come up with positive responses that challenge current Eeyore thinking, here's a great technique for strengthening this skill, which I learned via Brene Brown in her book *Dare to Lead*.[18] It's called 'the story I tell myself is…'.

The way it works is this. As soon as you – or others – come up with standard responses, such as, 'That won't work because… it isn't possible because… I can't (because), etc.',

Winning strategies

you reimagine the sentence by prefacing it with the phrase, 'the story I tell myself is...' which requires you to reveal to yourself and/or others the thought process that underpins this point of view.

Doing this enables you to consider the unspoken dialogue you hold in your mind that justifies current thinking and behaviour. It requires a willingness to be honest with yourself and others, yet it works in a way that feels strangely non-threatening. It enables vulnerability, an expression of inner thinking that is illuminating to all parties – and can lead to breakthroughs that are hard and slow to achieve in any other 'talking it out' process. Once mastered, this is a wonderful technique to use in the classroom and in meetings.

It gives us internal permission to reveal a part of ourselves that is routinely censured by the logical, pragmatic, rational mind. It bypasses the objections, providing a shortcut to reveal the previously hidden obstacles that really stand in the way of change or progress – that we can't even see for ourselves until we approach the thought in this way. Once we have answers revealed by this shortcut, then we can start to consider solutions that weren't previously available. Curiously, we are more willing to accept challenges to this 'story we tell ourselves' in ways we are not open to when we are challenged on the 'facts' which now reveal themselves as opinions. Practise on yourself. Practise with others. Practise at home. Practise at work.

Now you're ready to start coming up with positive and constructive alternatives. Just doing this will feel liberating.

Having come up with alternative ways of thinking, follow through with a new behaviour or action you can take that might lead towards a positive change. In my experience, this often means changing the nature of the conversation we have with others. This can mean overcoming assumptions and being open to a different response or outcome to the one which was part of 'the story we told ourselves'. In fact, repeatedly use the 'story I tell myself' to challenge all objections you present to yourself – or that others present to you. You will be surprised by the unexpected shifts that can occur by following this path, especially relating to your expectations of others. In my work with customers and clients, I never cease to be delighted and amazed when it's revealed that someone who would 'never' do x, suddenly does the unexpected.

Rinse and repeat. Continue creating ripples.

Learn to look for the detail in the solution

Continuing with the simple example above – where the problem is being stressed or anxious and the preferred state is calm and confident, you will need to become accomplished at reinforcing the positive state with examples.

In other words, you need to expand your repertoire of thinking about the solution with examples of just how that feels, what you might do differently if you felt that way, and situations where you might feel that, or have felt that in the past.

Senses are evocative of memory and emotion too. The more powerful the sense engaged, the more powerful the link to associated memory and associated emotion.

So when our imagination is stimulated (or even if it isn't), memory files within the brain are accessed, and any emotion associated with those memory files is replicated in the moment. Feelings will trump actions and logic for speed of access because they are the foundation stones of memory and understanding laid down in early childhood.

Winning strategies

To understand the power of this, bring your attention to how easily someone under stress (for whatever reason) can describe the problem. Given the opportunity, they can talk at length about the scale of the problem, evoking every tiny detail of how bad it is, thereby reinforcing the strength of the neural networks that drive and embed this way of thinking and feeling. And don't be fooled by an uncommunicative, sullen or acquiescent student or member of staff who says nothing.

Their thoughts will most definitely be dominated by turning over every tiny detail of what is wrong, what doesn't go well and how bad it could be. The truth is that this is exactly how their thinking will be going, even if they aren't saying it out loud.

On the path from novelty to mastery, the brain enjoys repetition and pattern matching and is ambivalent regarding good or bad, painful or enjoyable, positive or negative. When we're stuck in a negative place, this can seem frustrating and is the source of a plethora of self-help and therapeutic strategies. However, think of repetition as your friend. Just like learning any new skill, progress may be slow and difficult at the beginning. However, persist with seeking out the detail of every day, every experience, every interaction and, gradually, that repetition and neural pattern matching begins to work for you, rather than against you.

Aided by neuroplasticity, you begin to expand your capacity to see opportunity and positivity as a reflexive action. Keep at it and you will gain competence and, eventually, mastery.

The important things to pay attention to are the seemingly insignificant and unconnected moments of calm, happiness, enjoyment and pleasure, even if they seem transitory or irrelevant. In fact, the more transitory and irrelevant, the better. For example, if stress or low mood means the only tiny thing you notice that brings a small hint of pleasure is the sound of a bird, or the colour of a car, or the smile of a stranger, or a quiet thank you, the sound of rain, for example, then pay attention to it, make a mental note it. If you feel inclined or able, keep a physical note of it. This is a version of building what many people describe as mindfulness.

When I'm working directly with clients who struggle with anxiety, low mood or stress, many of them like to start a notebook, capturing these moments.

As you pay closer attention to doing this every day, what starts as a challenge with seemingly little to go on, starts to gather momentum. Your brain begins to get the hang of this and does one of the things it does best – pattern matching. So, your attention is drawn more frequently to other moments or memories that are triggered by the ones you are noticing. These connections may not be ones you would consciously make, but your mind works at a richer sensory level, so quickly presents you with more and more sensory-related matches.

We've all had moments when a fragrance, a colour, a momentary event or sound transports us to another time or place. This is exactly the process you are encouraging your mind to do more of – for your benefit. And it's happy to oblige.

Remember too, the 5:1 ratio required to tip the balance of thinking and feeling from negative to positive. Keep topping up your reserve of insignificant positive moments, so that you can draw on them when life inevitably throws a curveball, potentially knocking you off balance and preventing a return to old patterns of negative, stressful thinking.

There isn't a single curriculum subject or staff meeting where encouraging participants to consider preferable alternatives to things going wrong, or unwelcome events, would not be invaluable. It is a skill set that serves both individual and organisation well and sets them up for greater future success.

It's a core skill that underpins resilience.

Winning strategies

Mind your language

> But each time the conversation was freed from its pointless English shackles and allowed to fall back into the local tongues I would see it again, the clear sparks of intelligence – like flames licking through a grille meant to smother them – and taking the same form natural intelligence takes in classrooms around the world: backchat, humour, argument.[19]

This could honestly be the theme of an entire book. If anyone should know this, it would, you'd imagine, be a teacher. Language is powerful. Very powerful. You will know, of course, that it has the power to uplift, to inspire, to persuade, to manipulate, to inform, that it is a vital tool for communication and each and every one of your profession dedicates most of their waking hours to disseminating mastery of it, in order to support student learning and their progress through various career pathways, not to mention passing a few standard assessment tests (SATs) along the way. You'd think, therefore, that this was one area where I might agree with metrics and measurement. But no.

Privately, I believe most of us could do better when it comes to mastery of syntax, grammar and punctuation. However, my interest in language goes deeper than that. It should come as no surprise that a tool as powerful as language would play a major supporting role in the mental wealth of all of us. Language is so much more than a string of words in a sentence. It carries more than information. Language is power and emotion. It is both the tool of solution-focused, logical and rational thinking, considering, evaluating and disseminating ideas via the prefrontal cortex of your brain; and the very tip of an emotional iceberg that is accessed via your reticular activating system. A single word or phrase is attached to a myriad of associated meanings linked to experience, which is unique to the listener. We use shared language as a common tool, making an implicit assumption that the meaning we intend to convey is the meaning received. Any misunderstanding or miscommunication might be put down to a failure to appreciate the true dictionary meaning of a word. Yet, even as you read this, you are already aware that this is not the case. When it comes to the spoken word in particular, misunderstanding and miscommunication have little to do with dictionary definitions or appropriate use of syntax and grammar. There is also associated sensory information that the brain (yours *and* mine *and* theirs) interprets unconsciously according to prior experience. The brain, metaphorically speaking, draws on the vast search engine of its database (larger than Google) for what I describe as 'pattern matches'. In less than a second, the brain will find the closest match for how to behave in response to this particular experience and this piece of communicated information.

Your intention has nothing to do with how any recipient responds unless there is a pattern within the mind which defines the way you convey your intention as a match for a different pattern.

This may sound obscure but stick with it. You know that none of us speaks without intonation, accent, expression or body language, however slight or imperceptible to the conscious mind. It is these subtle variations, combined or separate, that contribute to another person's understanding and interpretation of meaning.

We know that we can observe this in part, with one of those sentence structures that changes its meaning according to where we place the emphasis. For example: 'She isn't flying to Dublin tomorrow'. Try emphasising a different word in this sentence each time you say it. Here's what happens[20]:

103

Winning strategies

- By emphasising the 'she' it implies that it is someone else that is flying to Dublin tomorrow.
- The 'isn't' shows that she's not doing this anymore.
- Emphasising the 'flying' means that she's not flying, she may be getting there another way instead.
- 'To' this could mean she is flying from or by Dublin not to.
- Emphasis on Dublin shows that it could be a different location, not Dublin.
- Finally, 'tomorrow' could mean that it's actually a different day, not tomorrow.

This shift in meaning can be fairly readily interpreted within the slower functioning, logical, conscious mind, our prefrontal cortex. Take the meaning deeper and you will appreciate that subtle inflections of tone, gesture or body language can shift meaning again, this time at the quicker responding subconscious level, which maps the experience onto previous experiences and triggers an associated behaviour. This behaviour makes perfect sense to the emotional mind because its only concern is safety. However, it might be behaviour that the originator of the communication associates with a different meaning, thereby setting up a communication impasse or conflict.

Again, as a teacher, you might be more mindful than most of the potential for miscommunication through language and other communication tools of body language, tone and gesture.

However, think of the impact of repetitive language patterns, language that is in habitual use within a school or a classroom, where the intent may be one thing but the received communication is one that is damaging to a person's mental fitness.

For example, 'these are the most important decisions of your lives' (trying to get young people to think deeply and choose 'wisely' when it comes to their exam, career or education choices). This kind of phrase can become a teacher and parent mantra which begins in Year 10 and continues through to Year 13. However, it is loaded with emotion and here is where the danger lies.

A young person who has built up a good stock of mental wealth, including resilience (see Chapter 3: Resilience Propaganda), may find this constructive and motivational because it reminds them to take time over their decision, to think through potential pros, cons and as many variable outcomes as possible. It may encourage them to seek additional professional guidance and advice in support of their own decisions until they reach the point where they feel they possess sufficient high-quality information to make a reasoned judgement. Seriously? How many young people do you think possess this amount of self-assurance, wisdom and balanced introspection, especially when the neuroscience says teenagers are predisposed to risk-based behaviour and struggle with consequential thinking? Some may be good at faking it – and they *are* faking it – based on acute observation and adherence to 'acceptable behaviour' and based on 'fitting in' or 'not standing out'. They will take the easy, non-conflict-inducing, conforming route with teachers and/or parents. But each of those reasons suggests they are at high risk of compromised mental well-being. Avoidance of conflict, fitting in, conforming, doing what's acceptable – are not the behaviours of confident, well-adjusted, young people, looking forward to fulfilling their potential according to what they want and living happy fulfilled lives. They are the behaviours of anxious, hypervigilant, nervy young people, usually marked out as high performers. They are trouble-free for the adults around them, but are most at risk of some of the more severe signs of mental distress, including depression, self-harm, eating disorders, OCD and suicidal thoughts. They may be unlikely to confide in people who can help them until

Winning strategies

their problems are pretty entrenched and this damaged way of thinking and behaving has serious implications for their entire adult life. I have personally met and worked with thousands of such individuals, who seem outwardly to have it all, but are consumed with self-doubt and low self-esteem, which negatively impacts on their happiness at work, their adult relationships and, eventually, their own children. And one of the key triggers is an innocent, but careless, use of language, such as, 'These are the most important decisions of your lives'.

Phrases with similar potential for damaging impact include, 'You'll never (fill in the blank) if you don't pass this exam/get this grade'. It isn't improved by shifting the emphasis from stick to carrot, such as, 'People with good grades in (fill in the blank) get better jobs'.

The more stress and pressure an individual is under, the more negatively powerful these phrases become. Stressed, anxious people play out worst case scenarios repeatedly in their head, based on what might happen, what might not happen, what they wish *had* happened or *hadn't* happened. None of those thoughts are constructive or helpful. And each negatively played out thought feeds more of the same till they get sucked into a downward vortex of feeling helpless and scared and infinitely worse than they should. Plus, a stressed member of staff may compound this by sharing their own worst case future scenario stories in a misplaced attempt to motivate those who appear outwardly stubborn or reluctant to engage seriously. In truth, both staff member and student are probably scared witless and their primitive brain is triggered with fear, so they can't think straight. Any such teacher rant or lecture, however, is not motivational. It is not helpful. It is not necessary. At best it is innocent, albeit misplaced encouragement. At worst, it is manipulative, sloppy and careless.

Sure, share the potential benefits of higher grades or exam passes in terms of university acceptance or specific career paths. *However*, make sure you are rock solid in your confidence that what you are sharing is truth rather than popularly held opinion.

What to do instead? Stay focused on the task in hand. Remain curious in such a way that the curiosity is contagious. *Always* include the caveat that there are other options and other ways to succeed. Ask students who they admire and why. Don't shy away from the conversation if they admire someone who dropped out of school or failed in education (but succeeded in life anyway). Maybe set a personal challenge to research the person they admire, and the path they took, including the key aspects which enabled them to get where they are or that they regret. If you look deeper, there will be lessons around the kind of qualities, persistence, commitment and courage that are aspirational and students can be encouraged to come up with ways they could hone those particular skills (which might be by showing up in school and getting work done to the best of their ability).

Final words

Mental wealth building is a lot like teaching. To get really good at it, you need to practise listening, ask great questions and let go of the need to be right. You need to encourage others to discover what's great about them and what they're good at. You need to help them celebrate themselves, take some calculated risks and trust themselves more. You need to shine a light on possibility till they feel bold enough to step into something bigger than they believed possible. As a courageous leader in secondary education, this is your moment to fall in love with teaching again.

Winning strategies

Rather than a 'nice to have' add-on policy, make long-term mental well-being for all your singular focus, so that every decision and policy flows from it. If you do nothing else, do that. Let go of the need to be 'right' too. Remember, there is no right or wrong, no 'this always works' or 'that never works'. Take some risks and break some rules of your own. Lead your team and your school by example. Be openly vulnerable. Be courageous. Be willing to fail.

Failure and the willingness to risk failure are the key tenets of success. Ask any entrepreneur. More is learned from 10 failures than 10 successes, if we are encouraged to feel bold enough to take those risks.

Question your own rules and boundaries. Are they enabling or disabling? If they're enabling, be crystal clear about what they are and why they matter, so that everyone understands.

Take more time to think when you think you have no time. Slow down.

Mentally healthy people are questioning, so don't shut them down when they ask why, or they challenge. Be better at listening than speaking.

Allow for flexibility as often as you can, because mental well-being doesn't come from securely locked doors. It comes from sights set on horizons and gates that open when you feel safe to move on.

Heap praise upon the person who gets it wrong, but can come up with a fresh approach based on learning from that failure. Encourage young people who always get it 'right' to risk getting it wrong.

It is not beyond the creativity of you or your staffing team to come up with innovative ways to apply any of this within the classroom. Teachers are creative people who crave the opportunity to express that more. Give them – and yourself – some freedom of operation, to enable a school culture which is less about people pleasing, or striving for acceptability, and more about 'colouring outside the lines' of rigid curriculum or tradition when it comes to unlocking personal potential.

Remember how creative you were when you first qualified, how each newly qualified teacher arrives brimming with the same kind of enthusiasm? Take yourself and each of them through a process of learning to love failure and wait for the results to start showing.

Staff will remain more engaged, the fire of their enthusiasm kindled and this will lower the high attrition rate as well as inspire students who had, till now, either been bored and disengaged, or too well behaved and lacking in any capacity to take risks (all of which has been systematically impoverishing their long-term mental health).

Growth is a journey paved with trial and error, not a one-stop destination. Each school has its own nuances, its own structural makeup and personalities which alter it each term and each academic year that staff and students come and go.

Do not accept a one-size-fits-all solution for your school. Be as discerning in your choice of what works here as you would be for yourself. At the same time, do your best to remain objective, to practice 'empty vessel' thinking and put your own biases and prejudices aside, in your leadership.

Of course you won't implement or agree with every single suggestion. You wouldn't be the creative, innovative maverick this book is aimed for if you did. However, you will use this as a springboard for progressive change that lies at the heart of your school success.

It's bigger than your personal CV. I like to think you're more about longer-term benefits for all, than simply your own incremental salary hikes for ticking the current 'on trend' boxes. Not that there's anything wrong with wanting to make more money; but if

Winning strategies

you came into teaching with the intention of changing lives for the better, you will need to be reminded of that repeatedly as you craft your plan and roll out your collaborative strategy with students, staff, governors and parents.

Make it a personal mantra, an unwavering goal that you will not surrender, come hell or high water – and our children might just stand a chance in the world evolving around them. They might just thank you. You will, I hope, thank yourself. Deservedly so.

Notes

1 https://curriculumsolutions.net/blog/2018/02/28/culturally-responsive-teaching-how-the-brain-can-hijack-learning/.
2 Wells, Barlow and Stewart-Brown, 2003, p. 14. www.mentalhealth.org.uk/sites/default/files/lifetime_impacts.pdf.
3 Source: www.health.harvard.edu/staying-healthy/understanding-the-stress-response.
4 Source: Halcyon Education podcast, https://halcyon.education/podcasts, 2019.
5 www.annafreud.org/5steps/.
6 www.annafreud.org/schools-and-colleges/5-steps-to-mental-health-and-well-being-background-and-user-guide/.
7 www.gov.uk/government/consultations/transforming-children-and-young-peoples-mental-health-provision-a-green-paper/quick-read-transforming-children-and-young-peoples-mental-health-provision.
8 Benjamin Hardy, *Personality Isn't Permanent*, 2020, Penguin Random House.
9 Source: https://journals.sagepub.com/doi/abs/10.1177/1098300717753831.
10 Source: www.edutopia.org/article/welcoming-students-smile.
11 Source: Joseph Bikart, *The Art of Decision Making*, 2019, Watkins.
12 Source: Clare Josa, *Ditching Imposter Syndrome*, 2019, Beyond Alchemy Publishing.
13 Source: John Tierney and Roy F. Baumeister, *The Power of Bad: And How to Overcome It*, 2019, Allen Lane.
14 Source: Andrea García Cerdán, translated by Alejandra Salazar, https://blog.cognifit.com/mirror-neurons/.
15 Source: https://youtu.be/vTylNRr1RZM.
16 Source: https://ohmy.disney.com/movies/2013/09/17/12-amazing-witticisms-from-eeyore/.
17 Source: https://ohmy.disney.com/movies/2013/09/17/12-amazing-witticisms-from-eeyore/.
18 Source: Brene Brown, *Dare to Lead*, 2018, Vermilion.
19 Source: Zadie Smith, *Swing Time*, 2016, Hamish Hamilton.
20 Source: https://eurotalk.com/blog/2015/10/30/taking-the-stress-test-how-emphasis-can-change-meaning.

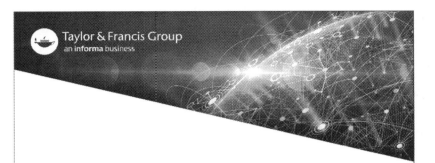

Printed in the United States
by Baker & Taylor Publisher Services